shortstory

shortstory
chic knits for layering

CATHY CARRON

sixth&spring

NEW YORK

sixth&spring books

161 Avenue of the Americas, New York, NY 10013

Editorial Director
JOY AQUILINO

Senior Editor
MICHELLE BREDESON

Yarn Editor
RENEE LORION

Instructions Editors
PAT HARSTE
BARBARA KHOURI

Instructions Proofreaders
CHARLOTTE PARRY
JUDITH SLOAN

Copy Editor
LISA SILVERMAN

Technical Illustrations
ULI MONCH

Photography
ROSE CALLAHAN

Stylist & Bookings Manager
SARAH LIEBOWITZ

Hair and Makeup
ELENA LYAKIR

Vice President, Publisher
TRISHA MALCOLM

Creative Director
JOE VIOR

Production Manager
DAVID JOINNIDES

President
ART JOINNIDES

Library of Congress Control Number: 2012937689
ISBN: 978-1-936096-45-9

Manufactured in China
1 3 5 7 9 10 8 6 4 2
First Edition

acknowledgments

Short Story is the third book in what is turning out to be a series. The process gets easier each time because the team at Sixth&Spring Books works as a finely tuned machine under the guidance of publisher Trisha Malcolm. The gears that make my world work there are Renée Lorion, once yarn master, now technical advisor, and my editor, Michelle Bredeson, whose forbearance during my wackier moments is noted and much appreciated. Not to be forgotten are the people who take my work and make visual magic: Joe Vior, the creative director, and stylist Sarah Liebowitz. Technical editors Pat Harste, Barbara Khouri, Judy Sloan, and Charlotte Parry ensured that the instructions are error free and easy to follow. Kudos to you all!

Except for the yarn credits in the back of each book, I have never explicitly thanked the folks at the yarn companies who've kindly supplied all the yummy fibers for this and my earlier books. It's understood that yarn companies work with designers to get exposure for their products. However, the grace and speed with which the stuff comes through the door is much appreciated. I'd especially like to call out Tricia Anderson of Tanglewood Fiber Creations in Oregon. Trish makes extraordinary yarns, and is also one of the most personable and enthusiastic people in the business. Another shout-out goes to Eugene Wyatt of Catskill Merino Sheep Farm. I inadvertently stumbled upon Eugene's yarn while rushing through the Union Square Greenmarket in New York City. I grabbed his card and made a point of contacting him, because he makes amazing yarns, and because I am a strong proponent of the locally grown movement. To him, and to all the yarn makers who contributed to this book, I am grateful.

contents

introduction
Short Is Sweet

After designing hats for heads **(Hattitude)** and cowls for necks **(Cowl Girls)**, it just seemed logical to work my way down to covers for shoulders, hence the focus for **Short Story**. Aside from the logical progression, there were many other reasons this type of collection appealed to me. First off, I really like to have my neck and shoulders protected no matter the season. Of course, during colder weather there's always that need for a little extra something, whether I'm inside or out. While padding around our house in the hills, I don't always want to carry around the bulk of a full sweater, so I'll toss on an extra little capelet or cropped top to protect me from drafts. Even in warm weather, I'm apt to wrap unless it's truly sauna-like outside. Summer nights in northwestern Connecticut can be chilly. And the ubiquity of air conditioning necessitates keeping some kind of shoulder covering on hand; while shopping during warmer months or in warmer climes, I often feel as if I am walking into a refrigerator rather than a store! Short tops and sweaters are just the thing.

Another appeal of short tops is their versatility. The opportunities for creative variations in shape, stitch patterns, and fiber are endless. As you'll see in the photos throughout this book, there is an almost infinite number of ways to style these abbreviated delights. And finally, short is sweet in both time and money: Smaller projects cost less and take less time, so instant gratification is just around the corner. Because fit is not critical for a number of projects, such as the ponchos, they would make ideal gifts. Of course the sweetest gift is often the one you give yourself, so pick your favorite and start knitting!

brief encounter:
a quick look at short tops

Button-Front
Cardi
(page 82)

Striped Pullover
(page 26)

Cashmere Shrug
(page 58)

For this collection, I've tried to come up with as many creative variations on the short top as possible. There are thirty-five designs included here. Before we get started knitting, here is a look at the various forms I've explored, yarn and stitch pattern considerations, advice for adjusting length, and ideas for styling short knits.

The Short Form

There's a plethora of options for constructing short tops. Top-down is my favorite method and is well represented here in both pullovers and cardigans. Other designs are knit from the bottom up and joined under the arms or knit flat and seamed. Below, I describe some basic shapes I've included in this collection. Don't get hung up on traditional definitions, though. Many designs in this book defy categorization. After all, pushing the boundaries is part of the fun of creating something yourself.

• Cardigans

James Thomas Brudenell, the 7th Earl of Cardigan, probably had no idea how long the sweater that bears his name would stay in style. Buttoned, tied, or left open, cardigans are the epitome of classic style. Cropping them keeps them modern and fresh.

• Pullovers

Cropped pullovers are carefree dressing at its best. Layer them over tanks, T-shirts, or even dresses for a casual, yet fashion-forward look. Knit "T-shirts" elevate the humble everyday topper to new levels of sophistication.

• Shrugs

A classic shrug is the shortest of short tops, sometimes no more than sleeves connected by a back portion. The usual way to construct one is to knit from sleeve to sleeve. I've created a few different versions for this book, including a cashmere shrug with dropped-stitch sleeves (page 58) and a bold Fair Isle number knit in bulky yarn (page 110).

• Ponchos

I had a lot of fun with shortened ponchos, or "ponchettes" if you will, in this book. Because the ponchos here are short, I was able to make some of them more fitted without restricting arm movement. Longer ponchos would need to be more fluid or feature slits in the sides to accommodate the arms.

• Boleros

Somewhere between a cardigan and shrug, a bolero is a waist-length sweater or jacket that is open at the front and named for a Spanish dance. I had a lot of fun with the bolero shape in this collection and designed a number of variations, including a ruffled bolero knit in handpainted yarns (page 38) that's fit for a fiesta and a chunky one made up of knitted squares joined together (page 70).

• Wraps

Nothing could be simpler, construction-wise, than a wrap. Whether knit as a simple rectangle (sort of an oversized scarf) or joined to hug the shoulders, a wrap is an essential item year round. For this collection, I added a cuff at one end of a long wrap (page 22) to slip over the arm and keep your hands free for dancing or mingling at a cocktail party.

A Good Yarn

There are no limits to the types of yarn that can be used to create cropped tops. I tried to use a wide variety in this collection to showcase the possibilities. Of course, classic worsted and DK-weight yarns are featured prominently. They create a medium-weight fabric ideal for multi-seasonal tops. Several pieces make good use of bulky yarns, which lend drama and extra thickness to chilly-weather warmers. In addition to gorgeous wool and alpaca yarns, I couldn't resist experimenting with yummy mohair, whimsical bouclé, glitzy metallic, cool cotton, fuzzy chenille, and glamorous beaded yarns. The list goes on and on. Sometimes the yarn inspires the design, such as the Cowlneck Capelet (page 78), in which the simple shape lets the hand-spun, hand-dyed yarn shine. Other times, the form comes first; for the Wide-Collar Ribbed Pullover (page 14), I wanted a bulky, multi-colored effect, so I held together three strands of worsted weight yarn in different colors. Don't be afraid to explore all options for a really fun knitting experience.

Ribbed Poncho
(page 50)

Ruffled Bolero
(page 38)

Cuffed Wrap
(page 22)

Striped Lace
Pullover
(page 126)

Patchwork
Bolero
(page 70)

Drop-Stitch
Poncho
(page 122)

In Stitches

Why always settle for simple stockinette or garter stitch when there are so many fabulous lace, cable, and other stitch patterns you can incorporate into your designs? When it comes to stitch patterns, I try to restrain my choices, usually limiting the number of patterns to no more than three per project. It's not a hard-and-fast rule, but it helps keep the design from looking too discombobulated. Of course there are exceptions to every rule. For the Striped Lace Pullover (page 126), there are six different lace patterns to keep you on your toes; alternating stripes of dark and medium blue tie them together.

Go the Distance

Not every design in this book will suit every body type or personal style. No doubt, there will be some you'll look at and think, "I like it, but I'd like it even better if it were longer." That's okay; many of the designs can be easily extended. One of the primary reasons I love the top-down method of garment construction is that such an alteration is easy; all you have to do is continue knitting the body until it reaches the desired length. (Just make sure you have enough yarn on hand!) Ponchos can be extended, but you'll probably want to make some kind of armhole in order to be able to manipulate your arms. Wraps can always be made longer too, just keep knitting. For a modular design such as the Patchwork Bolero on page 70, just add more motifs on the bottom body edge. For garments that are worked from the bottom up, decide before you start knitting if you want to add length, so you don't bump into any problems at the armholes.

Of course, a number of designs in this collection cannot be elongated, or would be difficult to lengthen. It's unlikely, for example, that you'd want to lengthen a shrug (such as the Bulky Fair Isle Shrug on page 110) that is worked from side to side; if so, you'd need to pick up stitches along the lower body edge and work down.

Make a Long Story Short

You might also find yourself asking, "Can I just 'chop' any knit design to get a cropped look?" You usually can, but you should first try to visualize how it would look (use a piece of paper to cover the bottom half of the photo!) and decide whether the original design would look good cropped or should be left as it was originally intended to be. Most important, determine whether you can easily change the pattern to shorten the design.

Read through the pattern to see how it is constructed. Top-down knits are the easiest to adjust; simply stop knitting when you reach the length you like. For sweaters that are knit from the bottom up or knit flat and seamed, decide in advance if you are going to adjust the design before you start knitting.

How to Get Layered

Other than the knitting, the real fun of short tops is wearing them. To me, short tops are like frosting. Most cakes can be eaten without frosting, but, as I'm sure you'll agree, it's the frosting that really makes the cake. Ditto for short tops and wraps. When you go out the door in the morning, you've got to be clothed; you really do need to minimally cover yourself with a pair of pants or skirt and a shirt or a dress. But anything beyond the basics is frosting. It's not really necessary to throw another smaller piece on top, but it can certainly make an ordinary get-up special.

Layering can enhance your figure, add more color and texture to an outfit, provide extra warmth (and the option to remove a layer if it gets too warm), and create a truly unique look. Light- to midweight pullovers and cardigans can be worn as an outer layer or a middle layer. Bulky cardigans take the place of a jacket on cool days. Of course, ponchos are best worn on top, but can be accessorized with scarves, gloves, or arm warmers (the Drop-Stitch Poncho on page 122 features matching ones!).

Any kind of light shirt—tanks, camisoles, T-shirts, polos—can work as a base layer to a cropped style. The key is to coordinate color, print, and proportion. Dresses are also fabulous base layers, and short pullovers look especially fresh over them. Although shawls and wraps are typical evening cover-ups, why not knit up a metallic cropped cardigan to wear instead (see the Tie-Front Cardi on page 18). Play with your pieces in front of the mirror to see what works. Mix it up and don't be afraid to take risks.

The Next Chapter

Finishing a collection doesn't stop me from coming up with more ideas, and I hope you'll use the designs in this book as a starting point for your own creativity. Consider customizing single-color or single-stitch designs with color blocking or "texture" blocking . . . add beads to necklines, hems, or cuffs . . . use two strands of yarn held together . . . substitute different stitches entirely. Be creative, and have fun!

out of the blue

Combining several shades of blue and green in one design takes "true blue" to a new level.

out of the blue

Yarn
Cascade 220 **by Cascade Yarns, 3½oz/100g hanks, each approx 220yd/201m (Peruvian highland wool)** [4]
• **2 (3, 3, 3) hanks each in #9421 blue hawaii, #8894 christmas green, and #9485 kentucky blue**

Needles
• **Two size 13 (9mm) circular needles, 24"/60cm long,** or size to obtain gauge
• **One set (5) size 13 (9mm) double-pointed needles (dpns)**

Notions
• **Stitch holders**
• **Stitch markers**

Skill Level
●●●○

WIDE-COLLAR RIBBED PULLOVER
It's hard to decide what's more fun, making this sweater or wearing it. Three strands of worsted yarn held together create a bulky, multicolored yarn. I combined shades of blue and green for a subtle blend, but you can experiment to create your own custom colorways!

SIZES
Instructions are written for size Small. Changes for Medium, Large, and X-Large are in parentheses. (Shown in size Small.)

FINISHED MEASUREMENTS
Bust 35¾ (37¾, 40, 42¾)"/91 (96, 101.5, 108.5)cm
Length 13 (13½, 14, 14¾)"/33 (34, 35.5, 37.5)cm
Upper arm 15 (15¾, 16½, 17)"/38 (40, 42, 43)cm

GAUGE
14 sts and 17 rows to 5"/12.5cm over k1, p1 rib using 3 strands of yarn held tog and size 13 (9mm) circular needle (slightly stretched). **Take time to check gauge.**

NOTES
1) Top is worked in one piece from the neckband down.
2) Use 1 strand of each color held tog.
3) You will be establishing k1, p1 rib on first inc row. Work rib over left front, left sleeve, back, right sleeve, then right front without interruption.
4) Work new sts in rib as sts become available.
5) Schematic is on page 154.

PULLOVER
Neckband
With circular needle and 1 strand of each color held tog, cast on 32 (32, 34, 36) sts. Working back and forth on 2 needles, cont as foll:
Next row (RS) Knit. **Next row** Purl.
Yoke
Next row (RS) K 2 sts (left front), pm, k6 sts (left sleeve), pm, k 16 (16, 18, 20) sts (back), pm, k6 sts (right sleeve), pm, k2 sts (right front).
Next row Purl across, slipping markers.
Please see Note and read through next 2 rows before beg.
Inc row (RS) *Work in k1, p1 rib to 1 st before next marker, yo, k1, slip marker, k1, yo; rep from * across 3 times more, work in rib to end—40 (40, 42, 44) sts.
Next row *Work in established rib pat to 1

st before next marker, p1, slip marker, p1; rep from * across 3 times more, work in rib to end. Rep last 2 rows 17 (18, 19, 20) times more. AT THE SAME TIME, inc 1 st each neck edge on second inc row, then every 6th row 3 (4, 4, 5) times more. When all inc's have been completed, end with a WS row—184 (194, 204, 216) sts.
Divide for body and sleeves
Next rnd (RS) Holding right and left fronts side-by-side, pm on RH needle for beg of rnds, work in rib to first sleeve marker, drop marker, place next 42 (44, 46, 48) sts on holder for sleeve, pm for side marker, work in rib across back sts to next sleeve marker, drop marker, place next 42 (44, 46, 48) sts on holder for sleeve, pm for side marker, work in rib to end—100 (106, 112, 120) sts.
Side shaping
Next rnd Work around in rib.
Dec rnd Work in rib to 2 sts before first side marker, k2tog tbl, slip marker, k2tog, work in rib to 2 sts before second side marker, k2tog tbl, slip marker, k2tog, work in rib to end. Rep last 2 rnds twice more—88 (94, 100, 108) sts. Bind off loosely in rib.
Sleeves
With RS facing, dpn and 1 strand of each color held tog, work in rib over 42 (44, 46, 48) sts from sleeve holder, dividing sts over 4 needles. Join and pm for beg of rnd. Work in rib for 1 rnd. Bind off loosely in rib.

FINISHING
Neckband/collar
With RS facing, circular needle, and 1 strand of each color held tog, pick up and k 1 st in center bottom of neck opening, pm, pick up and k 36 (38, 40, 42) sts evenly spaced along right front neck, 6 sts across sleeve edge, 17 (17, 19, 21) sts across back neck edge, 6 sts across sleeve edge, then 36 (38, 40, 42) sts along left neck edge—102 (106, 112, 118) sts. Pm for beg of rnds.
Next rnd K center st, slip marker, p1, *k1, p1; rep from * around.
Dec rnd K center st, slip marker, k2tog tbl, work in rib to 2 sts before rnd marker, end k2tog. Rep last 2 rnds 5 (5, 6, 6) times more—90 (94, 98, 108) sts.
Next row (RS) K center st, drop marker, work in rib to end, drop rnd marker. Working back and forth on 2 needles, work even in rib for 7 (7, 7½, 7½)"/18 (18, 19, 19)cm. Bind off loosely in rib. ❖

tie one on

Get set to shine in this shimmering cardi with an elegant tie collar.

tie one on

WHAT YOU NEED

Yarn
Stella **by S. Charles Collezione/
Tahki•Stacy Charles**, .88oz/25g balls,
each approx 77yd/70m (silk/lurex)
• 14 (15, 17, 18) balls in #05 twilight

Needles
• One size 8 (5mm) circular needle,
29"/74cm long, or size to obtain gauge
• Two size 8 (5mm) circular needles,
16"/40cm long
• One set (4) size 8 (5mm) double-pointed
needles (dpns)

Notions
• Stitch markers
• Tapestry needle

Skill Level
●●●●

TIE-FRONT CARDI

Knit-in scarves are an easy way to lend a
charming, romantic look to a simple
shape, like this top-down cardi. **Stella**
yarn, a blend of silk and metallic
threads, adds some extra razzle-dazzle.

SIZES

Instructions are written for size Small.
Changes for Medium, Large, and
X-Large are in parentheses. (Shown in
size Small.)

FINISHED MEASUREMENTS

Back width at underarm 17¼ (18¾, 20¾,
22¾)"/44 (47.5, 52.5, 57.5)cm
Back length 8¾ (9½, 10½, 11¼)"/22 (24,
26.5, 28.5)cm

GAUGES

22 sts and 32 rows (rnds) to 4"/10cm over
St st using size 8 (5mm) needle.
30 sts and 32 rows (rnds) to 4"/10cm over
k1, p1 rib using size 8 (5mm) needle.
Take time to check gauges.

NOTES

1) Cardi is worked in one piece from the
top down.
2) Schematic is on page 154.

STITCH GLOSSARY

k2w Knit the st, wrapping yarn around
needle twice.
kf&b Inc 1 by knitting into the front and
back of the next st.

K1, P1 RIB

(over an odd number of sts)
Row 1 (WS) P1, *k1, p1; rep from *
across.
Row 2 (RS) K1, *p1, k1; rep from *
across.
Rep rows 1 and 2 for k1, p1 rib.

CARDI

Scarf/Collar
Using 29"/74cm circular needle, cast on
160 (165, 170, 175) sts and work back and
forth.
Rows 1 and 2 Knit.

Row 3 K2w 7 times, k to last 6 sts, k2w
to end.
Row 4 K across, dropping the wraps on
wrapped sts.
Row 5 Knit.
Row 6 K2w 15 times, k to last 6 sts, k2w
to end.
Row 7 K across, dropping the wraps on
wrapped sts.
Row 8 Knit.
Rep rows 3–8 6 times more.
Next row K2w 7 times, k to last 16 sts,
k2w to end.
Make scarf hole
Next row K20, bind off 12 sts, k to end.
Next row K across, casting on 12 sts
over bound-off sts.
Rep rows 3–8 7 times more.
Bind off 40 sts at the beg of next 2
rows—80 (85, 90, 95) sts.
Yoke
Row 1 (RS) K 18 (20, 21, 22) left front
sts, pm, k 9 sleeve sts, pm, k 26 (27, 30,
33) back sts, pm, k 9 sleeve sts, pm, k 18
(20, 21, 22) right front sts.
Row 2 (WS) P across, slipping markers.
Row 3 (inc row) (RS) (K1, yo) 17 (19, 20,
21) times, k1, sl marker, k9 sleeve sts, sl
marker, (k1, yo) 25 (26, 29, 32) times, k1, sl
marker, k9 sleeve sts, sl marker, (k1, yo) 17
(19, 20, 21) times, end k1; 35 (39, 41, 43)
sts each front and 51 (53, 59, 65) sts at
back—139 (149, 159, 169) sts.
Row 4 (WS) Work row 1 of k1, p1 rib to
marker, sl marker, p9, sl marker, work row
1 of k1, p1 rib to marker, sl marker, p9, sl
marker, work row 1 of k1, p1 rib to end.
Row (inc) 5 (RS) *Work in rib as est (k
the knit sts and p the purl sts) to 1 st
before marker, yo, k1, sl marker, k1, yo,
k to 1 st before next marker, yo, k1, sl
marker, k1, yo; rep from * once, work in
rib as est to end—147 (157, 167, 177) sts.
Row 6 (WS) Work across in est pats,
slipping markers and working all incs
each side of markers in St st (k on RS, p
on WS).
Row (inc) 7 (RS) *Work in rib and St st to
1 st before marker, yo, k1, sl marker, k1,
yo, k to 1 st before next marker, yo, k1, sl
marker, k1, yo; rep from * once, work in

St st and rib as est to end—155 (165, 175, 185) sts.

Row 8 (WS) Work across in est pats, slipping markers and working all incs each side of markers into St st.

Rep rows 7 and 8 27 (30, 34, 37) times more—371 (405, 447, 481) sts.

Divide yoke

Next row (RS) Work 64 (71, 77, 82) sts in est rib and St st to sleeve marker, slip 67 (73, 81, 87) sleeve sts onto a 16"/40cm circular needle and hold aside, continuing in k1, p1 rib and St st across 109 (117, 131, 143) back sts, slip 67 (73, 81, 87) sleeve sts onto 16"/40cm circular needle and hold aside, cont in k1, p1 rib and St st across 64 (71, 77, 82) right front sts—237 (259, 285, 307) sts remain.

Body

Rows 1–7 Work in est k1, p1 rib across, working a k2tog if necessary when working from a St st section to rib section to keep ribs in pat. Bind off in rib.

Sleeves

Divide 67 (73, 81, 87) sleeve sts evenly on 3 dpn, pm at underarm and join to beg work in the round.

Rnd 1 K2tog, k around—66 (72, 80, 86) sts.

Rnds 2–9 Knit.

Rnd 10 K2tog, k to last 2 sts, end k2tog-tbl—64 (70, 78, 84) sts.

Rnds 11–14 Knit.

Rep rnds 10–14 until 38 (40, 42, 42) sts remain.

Cuff

Next rnd *K2, yo, rep from * around—57 (60, 63, 63) sts.

Knit until cuff measures 5"/12.5cm.

Next rnd K2, *drop st, kf&b, k1; rep from * around, end kf&b in the first st of next rnd.

Bind off.

Rep for second sleeve.

FINISHING

Sew body and sleeves together at underarm. Gently ease out dropped stitches on both cuffs. ✤

grecian turn

Any way you wear it, you'll feel like a goddess
in this stunning mohair wrap.

grecian turn

WHAT YOU NEED

Yarn
Ritratto **by Stacy Charles, 1¾oz/50g hanks, each approx 198yd/180m (viscose/mohair/polyamide/polyester)**
• **1 hank in #126 blue hawaii (A)**
Luna **by Stacy Charles, .88oz/25g hanks, each approx 232yd/212m (super kid mohair/silk/lurex)** 2
• **8 (9, 9, 9) hanks in #25 blue moon (B)**

Needles
• **Size 8 (5mm) circular needle, 29"/74cm long,** or size to obtain gauge
• **Cable needle (cn)**

Notions
• **Stitch markers**

Skill Level
●●○○

CUFFED WRAP

This wrap was designed so that it could be worn and held in place without using your hands; slip your arm through the cuff and drape the wrap around your shoulders, or slip one end through the cuff to create a closed wrap.

SIZES

Instructions are written for size Small. Changes for Medium, Large, and X-Large are in parentheses. (Shown in size Small.)

FINISHED MEASUREMENTS

Cuff width 5"/12.5cm
Cuff circumference 11 (12, 13, 14)"/28 (30.5, 33, 35.5)cm
Scarf 25"/63.5cm x 57 (59, 61, 63)"/145 (150, 155, 160)cm

GAUGES

26 sts and 22 rows to 4"/10cm over chart pat 1 using 2 strands of A held tog and size 8 (5mm) circular needle.
19 sts and 20 rows to 4"/10cm over chart pat 2 using 2 strands of B held tog and size 8 (5mm) circular needle. **Take time to check gauges.**

NOTE

Use 2 strands of yarn held tog throughout.

STITCH GLOSSARY

Wrap 4 Knit 4, sl the last 4 sts worked onto cn, and wrap yarn once counterclockwise around these 4 sts; then sl the 4 sts back to RH needle.

kf&b Inc 1 by knitting into the front and back of the next st.

WRAP

Cuff
With 2 strands of A held tog, cast on 33 sts. Work back and forth as foll:
Beg chart pat 1
Row 1 (RS) Work first st, work 10-st rep 3 times, work last 2 sts. Cont to foll chart in this way to row 6, then rep rows 3–6 until piece measures 11 (12, 13, 14)"/28 (30.5, 33, 35.5)cm from beg or length that fits comfortably around arm above elbow, end with a WS row.
Shawl
Change to 2 strands of B held tog.
Next (inc) row (RS) Kf&b in each st across—66 sts.
Next row Purl.
Next (inc) row (RS) Kf&b in each st across—132 sts.
Next row Purl.
Beg chart pat 2
Row 1 (RS) Work first 17 sts, pm, work 7-st rep 14 times, pm, work last 17 sts. Slipping markers every row, cont to foll chart in this way to row 6, then rep rows 3–6 until piece measures 56½ (58½, 60½, 62½)"/143.5 (148.5, 153.5, 159)cm from beg, end with a WS row. Cont in garter st (knit every row) for 5 rows. Bind off loosely knitwise.

FINISHING

With WS tog, sew cast-on edge of cuff to last row of cuff using one strand of A. ❖

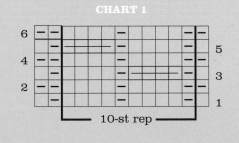

CHART 1

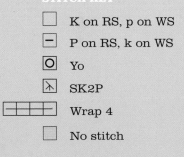

STITCH KEY

☐ K on RS, p on WS
− P on RS, k on WS
⦿ Yo
⅄ SK2P
⊞ Wrap 4
☐ No stitch

CHART 2

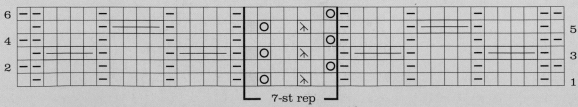

7-st rep

merry go round

Stripes of every color encircle your shoulders
in this dazzling topper.

merry go round

WHAT YOU NEED

Yarn
Worsted Hand Dyes **by Blue Sky Alpacas,
3½oz/100g hanks, each approx 100yd/91m
(royal alpaca/merino wool)**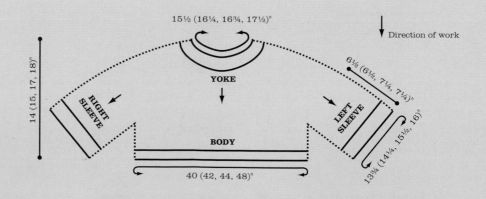
- **1 (1, 2, 2) hank in #2006 black (A)**
- **1 hank each in #2022 butterscotch (B),
#2007 light blue (C), #2000 red (D), #2025
charcoal (E), #2002 green (F), #2001
dungaree blue (G), #2008 light pink (H),
#2016 chocolate (I), #2010 rusty orange
(J), #2013 midnight blue (K), #2014 olive
(L), and #2012 cranberry (M)**

Needles
- **Size 9 (5.5mm) circular needles,
16"/40cm, 24"/61cm, and 29"/74cm long,** or
size to obtain gauge
- **One set (5) size 9 (5.5cm) double-pointed
needles (dpns)**

Notions
- **Stitch holders**
- **Stitch marker**

Skill Level
●●●●

STRIPED PULLOVER
I took one look at the color card for this
yarn and said, "I want them all!" Stripes
allow me to work as many colors as
possible into the mix, and the stitch pattern
keeps the striping from being ho-hum.

SIZES
Instructions are written for size Small.
Changes for Medium, Large, and X-Large
are in parentheses. (Shown in size Small.)

FINISHED MEASUREMENTS
Bust 40 (42, 44, 48)"/101.5 (106.5, 111.5,
122)cm
Length 14 (15, 17, 18)"/35.5 (38, 43,
45.5)cm (including collar)
Upper arm 13¾ (14¼, 15½, 16)"/35 (36,
39.5, 40.5)cm

GAUGE
19 sts to 4"/10cm and 33 rnds to 5"/12.5cm
over granite relief st using size 9 (5.5mm)
circular needle. **Take time to check gauge.**

NOTE
Top is worked in one piece from the collar
down.

STITCH GLOSSARY
kf&b Inc 1 by knitting into the front and
back of the next st.

GRANITE RELIEF STITCH
(over a multiple of 2 sts)
Rnd 1 Knit.
Rnd 2 *P2tog; rep from * around.
Rnd 3 *Kf&b; rep from * around.
Rnd 4 Knit.
Rep rnds 1-4 for granite relief st.

PULLOVER
Collar
With dpn and A, cast on 74 (77, 80, 84)
sts. Divide sts over 4 needles. Join, taking
care not to twist sts on needles; pm for beg
of rnds.
Next 22 rnds Purl. Change to 16"/40cm
circular needle.
Next (inc) rnd *K3, kf&b; rep from * around,
end k 2 (1, 0, 4)—92 (96, 100, 104) sts.
Yoke
Stripe 1
With B, work rnds 1–4 of granite relief st.
Stripe 2
With C, work as foll: **Next rnd** Knit.
Change to 24"/61cm circular needle.
Next (inc) rnd *K1, kf&b; rep from *
around—138 (144, 150, 156) sts. Work
rnds 2–4 of granite relief st.
Stripe 3
With D, work as foll: **Next rnd** Knit. Work
rnds 1–4 of granite relief st.
Stripe 4
With E, work as foll: **Next rnd** Knit.
Change to 29"/74cm circular needle.
Next (inc) rnd *K2, kf&b; rep from *
around—184 (192, 200, 208) sts. Work
rnds 2–4 of granite relief st.
Stripe 5
With F, work as foll: **Next rnd** Knit. Work
rnds 1–4 of granite relief st.
Stripe 6
With G, work as foll: **Next rnd** Knit.
Next (inc) rnd *K3, kf&b; rep from *
around—230 (240, 250, 260) sts. Work
rnds 2–4 of granite relief st.
Stripe 7
With H, work as foll: **Next rnd** Knit. Work
rnds 1–4 of granite relief st.
Stripe 8
With I, work as foll: **Next rnd** Knit.
Next (inc) rnd *K4, kf&b; rep from *
around—276 (288, 300, 312) sts. Work
rnds 2–4 of granite relief st.
Stripe 9
With J, work as foll: **Next rnd** Knit. Work
rnds 1–4 of granite relief st.

15½ (16¼, 16¾, 17½)"

Direction of work

14 (15, 17, 18)"

YOKE

RIGHT SLEEVE

LEFT SLEEVE

6½ (6½, 7¼, 7¼)"

BODY

13¾ (14¼, 15½, 16)"

40 (42, 44, 48)"

For size Small only
Stripe 10
With K, work as foll: **Next rnd** Knit.
Next (inc) rnd *K5, kf&b; rep from *
around—322 sts. Work rnds 2–3 **only** of
granite relief st.

For size Medium only
Stripe 10
With K, work as foll: **Next rnd** Knit.
Next (inc) rnd *K5, kf&b; rep from *
around—336 sts. Work rnds 2–4 of granite
relief st.
Stripe 11
With L, work as foll: **Next rnd** Knit. Work
rnds 1–3 *only* of granite relief st.

For size Large only
Stripe 10
With K, work as foll: **Next rnd** Knit.
Next (inc) rnd *K5, kf&b; rep from *
around—350 sts. Work rnds 2–4 of granite
relief st.
Stripe 11
With L, work as foll: **Next rnd** Knit. Work
rnds 1–4 of granite relief st.
Stripe 12
With E, work as foll: **Next rnd** Knit.
Next (inc) rnd *K34, kf&b; rep from *
around—360 sts. Work rnds 2–3 **only** of
granite relief st.

For size X-Large only
Stripe 10
With K, work as foll: **Next rnd** Knit.
Next (inc) rnd *K5, kf&b; rep from *
around—364 sts. Work rnds 2–4 of granite
relief st.
Stripe 11
With L, work as foll: **Next rnd** Knit. Work
rnds 1–4 of granite relief st.
Stripe 12
With E, work as foll: **Next rnd** Knit.
Next (inc) rnd [K21, kf&b, k22, kf&b] 8
times, end k4—380 sts. Work rnds 2–4 of
granite relief st.
Stripe 13
With F, work as foll:
Next rnd Knit. Work rnds 1–3 **only** of
granite relief st.

For all sizes
Divide for body and sleeves
With K (L, E, F), work as foll:
Next rnd K 96 (100, 106, 114) sts, place
next 66 (68, 74, 76) sts on holder for right
sleeve, k next 94 (100, 106, 114) sts, place
last 66 (68, 74, 76) sts on holder for left

sleeve—190 (200, 212, 228) sts. Join and
pm for beg of rnds.
Body
Stripe 1
With E (E, M, M), work as foll: **Next rnd**
Knit. Work rnds 1–4 of granite relief st.
Stripe 2
With M (M, C, C), work as foll: **Next rnd**
Knit. Work rnds 1–4 of granite relief st.
Stripe 3
With C (C, B, B), work as foll: **Next rnd**
Knit. Work rnds 1–4 of granite relief st.

For sizes Large and X-Large only
Stripe 4
With J, work as foll: **Next rnd** Knit. Work
rnds 1–4 of granite relief st.

For all sizes
With A, work as foll: **Next rnd** Knit.
Next (dec) rnd *K3, k2tog tbl; rep from *
around, end k 0 (0, 1, 1), k 0 (0, 1, k2tog
tbl)—152 (160, 170, 182) sts.
Next 5 rnds *K1, p1; rep from * around.
Bind off loosely in rib.

Right sleeve
With RS facing, dpn and K (L, E, F), k 66
(68, 74, 76) sts from holder, dividing sts
evenly over 4 needles.
Stripe 1
With C (C, L, L), work as foll:
Next rnd Knit. Join, taking care not to
twist sts on needles; pm for beg of rnds.
Work rnds 1–4 of granite relief st.
Stripe 2
With B (B, H, H), work as foll: **Next rnd**
Knit. Work rnds 1–4 of granite relief st.
Stripe 3
With M (M, C, C), work as foll: **Next rnd**
Knit. Work rnds 1–4 of granite relief st.
Stripe 4
With L (L, B, B), work as foll: **Next rnd**
Knit. Work rnds 1–4 of granite relief st.
Stripe 5
With H (H, M, M), work as foll: **Next rnd**
Knit. Work rnds 1–4 of granite relief st.

For sizes Large and X-Large only
Stripe 6
With J, work as foll: **Next rnd** Knit. Work
rnds 1–4 of granite relief st.

For all sizes
With A, work as foll: **Next rnd** Knit.
Next 10 rnds *K1, p1; rep from * around.
Bind off in rib.

Left sleeve
With RS facing, dpn, and K (L, E, F), k 66
(68, 74, 76) sts from holder, dividing sts
evenly over 4 needles.
Stripe 1
With D (D, I, I), work as foll:
Next rnd Knit. Join, taking care not to
twist sts on needles; pm for beg of rnds.
Work rnds 1–4 of granite relief st.
Stripe 2
With F (F, C, C), work as foll: **Next rnd**
Knit. Work rnds 1–4 of granite relief st.
Stripe 3
With B (B, D, D), work as foll: **Next rnd**
Knit. Work rnds 1–4 of granite relief st.
Stripe 4
With L (L, G, G), work as foll:
Next rnd Knit. Work rnds 1–4 of granite
relief st.
Stripe 5
With C (C, L, L), work as foll:
Next rnd Knit. Work rnds 1–4 of granite
relief st.

For Large and X-Large sizes only
Stripe 6
With B, work as foll:
Next rnd Knit. Work rnds 1–4 of granite
relief st.

For all sizes
With A, work as foll:
Next rnd Knit.
Next 10 rnds *K1, p1; rep from * around.
Bind off in rib.

FINISHING
Fold collar in half to WS and sew in
place. ✤

miss match

Stripes on one side and a lacy
texture on the other create a top that
tells both sides of the story.

miss match

WHAT YOU NEED

Yarn
Cotton Ease **by Lion Brand, 3½oz/100g
balls, each approx 207yd/188m
(cotton/acrylic)**
• 3 (4, 4, 5) balls in #099 almond (MC)
• 1 ball in #152 charcoal (CC)

Needles
• **Size 8 (5mm) circular needles, 16"/40cm
and 29"/74cm long,** or size to obtain gauge

Notions
• Stitch holders
• Stitch markers

Skill Level
●●●○

STRIPES AND LACE CROP TOP

I love the idea of combining different textures, patterns, or colors—or all of the above!—in one garment. This simple boxy top was done up with stripes on one side and a lacy pattern on the other, but because both sides share the same color palette, the look is unified, not kooky.

SIZES

Instructions are written for size Small. Changes for Medium, Large, and X-Large are in parentheses. (Shown in size Small.)

FINISHED MEASUREMENTS

Bust 46 (50, 54, 58)"/117 (127, 137, 147.5)cm
Length 15 (15½, 16, 16½)"/38 (39.5, 40.5, 42)cm

GAUGE

16 sts and 24 rows to 4"/10cm over St st using size 8 (5mm) circular needle. **Take time to check gauge.**

NOTE

When working stripe pat on front, do not carry CC up side edge. Instead, beg and end each CC stripe leaving a 5"/12.5cm tail. Weave in tails when front is completed.

K2, P2 RIB

(over a multiple of 4 sts plus 2)
Row 1 (RS) K2, *p2, k2; rep from * to end.
Row 2 P2, *k2, p2; rep from * to end.
Rep rows 1 and 2 for k2, p2 rib.

FEATHER FAGGOTING

(over a multiple of 4 sts)
Row 1 *K1, yo, p2tog, k1; rep from * to end.
Rep row 1 for feather faggoting.

STRIPE PATTERN

*Work 2 rows CC, 6 rows MC; rep from * (8 rows) for stripe pat.

BACK

With longer circular needle and MC, cast on 90 (98, 106, 114) sts. Work in k2, p2 rib for 8 rows, inc 2 sts evenly spaced across last row and end with a WS row— 92 (100, 108, 116) sts.
Next row (RS) K2, pm, work in feather faggoting to last 2 sts, pm, k2.
Next row K2, sl marker, work in feather faggoting to next marker, sl marker, k2. Keeping 2 sts each side in garter st (knit every row) and rem sts in feather faggoting, work even until piece measures 15 (15½, 16, 16½)"/38 (39.5, 40.5, 42)cm from beg, end with a WS row.
Shoulder shaping
Working in St st (knit on RS, purl on WS), bind off 24 (27, 30, 33) sts at beg of next 2 rows. Place rem 44 (46, 48, 50) sts on holder for back neck.

FRONT

With longer circular needle and MC, cast on 90 (98, 106, 114) sts. Work in k2, p2 rib for 8 rows, inc 2 sts evenly spaced across last row and end with a WS row— 92 (100, 108, 116) sts.
Next row (RS) K2, pm, knit to last 2 sts, pm, k2.
Next row K2, sl marker, purl to next marker, sl marker, k2. Keeping 2 sts each side in garter st and rem sts in St st, cont in stripe pat across all sts (including garter sts each side) and work even until piece measures same length as back to shoulder, end with a WS row. Shape shoulders as for back. Place rem 44 (46, 48, 50) sts on holder for front neck.

FINISHING

Sew shoulder seams.
Neck edging
With RS facing, shorter circular needle, and CC, beg at right shoulder seam and knit 44 (46, 48, 50) sts from back neck holder, then 44 (46, 48, 50) sts from front neck holder—88 (92, 96, 100) sts. Join and pm for beg of rnds. Purl 1 rnd, knit 1 rnd. Bind off loosely knitwise. Sew a 6"/15cm seam on each side. ❖

11 (11½, 12, 12½)"   6 (6¾, 7½, 8¼)"

9 (9½, 10, 10½)"

15 (15½, 16, 16½)"

**FRONT
&
BACK**

6"

23 (25, 27, 29)"

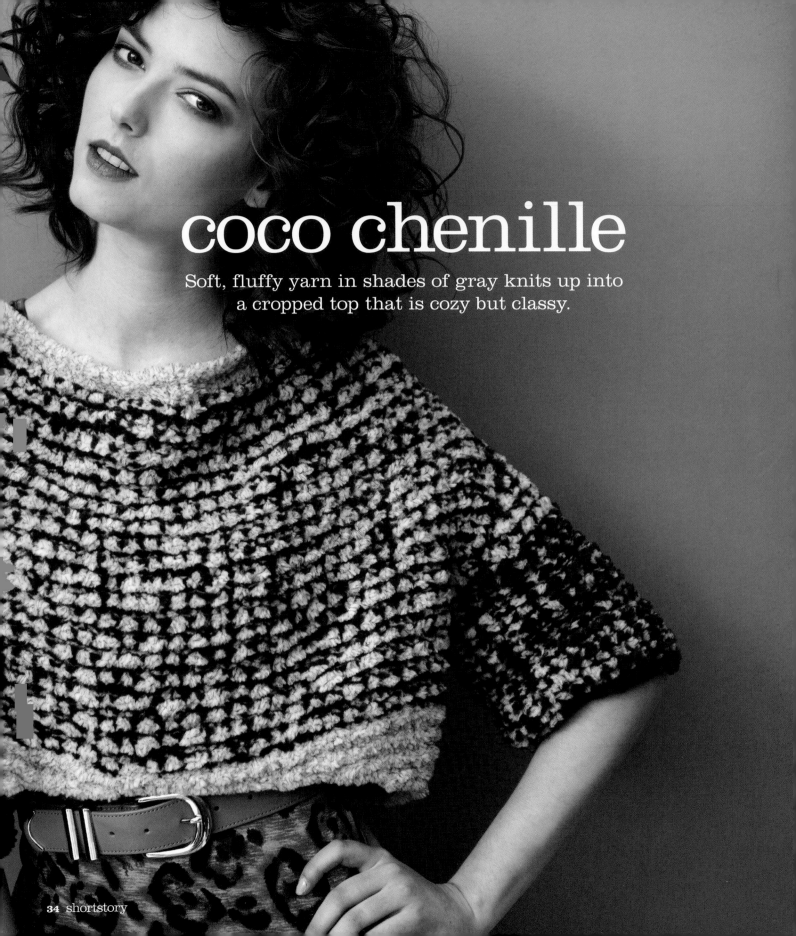

coco chenille

Soft, fluffy yarn in shades of gray knits up into
a cropped top that is cozy but classy.

coco chenille

WHAT YOU NEED

Yarn
Cincilla **by Filatura Di Crosa**, 1¾oz/50g balls, each approx 38yd/35m (wool/acrylic/polyamide)
- 4 (5, 5, 6) balls in #3 light grey (A)
- 4 (5, 5, 6) balls in #7 charcoal (B)

Needles
- **Two size 13 (9mm) circular needles, 24"/60cm long**, or size to obtain gauge
- **Size 13 (9mm) circular needle, 16"/40cm long**

Notions
- **Stitch holders**
- **Stitch marker**

Skill Level
●●●○

FAUX TWEED PULLOVER
The fun part of this design is that the same two tones of gray are combined to create two different tweedy patterns, just by switching which shade is knit and which is purled. It's a very simple idea, but it creates a fascinating effect.

SIZES
Instructions are written for size Small. Changes for Medium, Large, and X-Large are in parentheses. (Shown in size Small.)

FINISHED MEASUREMENTS
Bust 41 (44½, 48, 52½)"/104 (113, 122, 133.5)cm
Length 16 (16½, 18, 18½)"/40.5 (42, 45.5, 47)cm

Upper arm 16 (17, 18, 19½)"/40.5 (43, 45.5, 49.5)cm

GAUGE
7 sts and 14 rnds to 4"/10cm over ridged striping using size 13 (9mm) circular needle. **Take time to check gauge.**

NOTES
1) Top is worked in one piece from the neck down.
2) Schematic shows the front separated from the back and sleeves. Raglan armhole shaping is worked on back yoke and sleeves only. Front yoke is worked straight with no shaping.
3) Note that front is wider than back.

RIDGED STRIPING
Rnd 1 With A, knit.
Rnd 2 With B, purl.
Rep rnds 1 and 2 for ridged striping.

INVERSE RIDGED STRIPING
Rnd 1 With A, purl.
Rnd 2 With B, knit.
Rep rnds 1 and 2 for inverse ridged striping.

PULLOVER
Collar
With longer circular needle and A, cast on 56 (60, 64, 70) sts. Join, taking care not to twist sts on needle; pm for beg of rnds.
Rnds 1 and 2 Knit.
Rnd 3 With B, purl.
Rnd 4 With A, knit.
Rnd 5 With B, purl.
Yoke
Next rnd With A, k 38 (41, 44, 49) sts (front), pm, k4 sts (left sleeve), pm, k 10 (11, 12, 13) sts (back), pm, k4 sts (right sleeve).
Next (inc) rnd With B, purl to first marker

(front), sl marker, p1, yo, purl to 1 st before next marker (left sleeve), yo, p1, sl marker, p1, yo, purl to 1 st before next marker (back) yo, p1, sl marker, p1, yo, purl to 1 st before next marker (right sleeve), yo, p1— 62 (66, 70, 76) sts; 6 sts inc.
Next rnd With A, knit across, slipping markers. Rep last 2 rnds 11 (12, 13, 14) times more—128 (138, 148, 160) sts.
Next rnd With B, purl.
Dividing for body and sleeves
Next rnd With A, k 38 (41, 44, 49) front sts, place next 28 (30, 32, 34) sts on holder for left sleeve, k 34 (37, 40, 43) back sts, place rem 28 (30, 32, 34) sts on holder for right sleeve—72 (78, 84, 92) sts. Join and pm for beg of rnds. Cont with rnd 2, work even in ridged striping for 3½ (3½, 4½, 4½)"/9 (9, 11.5, 11.5)cm, end with rnd 2. Cut yarns.
Bottom band
Create a new starting point by placing first 19 (20, 22, 24) sts of front onto RH end of needle. Rejoin A.
Next rnd With A, knit.
Next rnd With B, purl.
Band shaping
Cont with A only, work as foll:
Row 1 (RS) Bind off first 6 sts, knit to end. Turn work. Working back and forth using 2 longer needles, cont as foll:
Row 2 Bind off first 6 sts, knit to end.
Rows 3–8 Bind off first 3 sts, knit to end.
Bind off rem 42 (48, 54, 62) sts loosely knitwise.
Sleeves
With RS facing, shorter circular needle and A, p 28 (30, 32, 34) sts from sleeve holder. Join and pm for beg of rnds. Beg with rnd 2, cont in inverse ridged striping for 6½ (6½, 7, 7)"/16.5 (16.5, 18, 18)cm, end with rnd 2. Bind off loosely knitwise using B. ❧

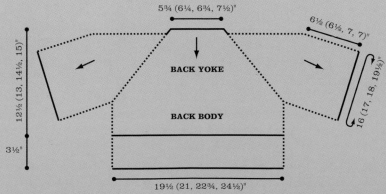

5¾ (6¼, 6¾, 7½)"
6½ (6½, 7, 7)"
12½ (13, 14½, 15)"
BACK YOKE
BACK BODY
16 (17, 18, 19½)"
3½"
19½ (21, 22¾, 24½)"

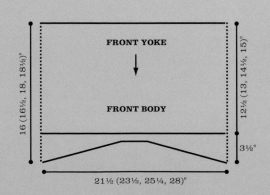

FRONT YOKE
FRONT BODY
16 (16½, 18, 18½)"
12½ (13, 14½, 15)"
3½"
21½ (23½, 25¼, 28)"

painter's palette

Gorgeous handpainted yarns provide a
rainbow of colors to top off any look.

painter's palette

WHAT YOU NEED

Yarn
Handpaint Chunky **by Misti Alpaca**, 3½oz/100g hanks, each approx 109yd/100m (baby alpaca) **5**
• 3 (4, 4, 4) hanks in #CP10 fox tail (A)
• 4 (5, 5, 5) hanks in #CP20 macbeth (B)
Chunky **by Misti Alpaca**, 3½oz/100g hanks, each approx 109yd/100m (baby alpaca) **5**
• 1 hank in #2L470 black cream (C)

Needles
• Size 10 (6mm) circular needles, 29"/74cm and 36"/91cm long, or size to obtain gauge
• One set (4) size 10 (6mm) double-pointed needles (dpns)

Notions
• Stitch holders
• Stitch markers

Skill Level
●●●○

RUFFLED BOLERO

Every colorway of Misti Alpaca's **Handpaint Chunky** is so fabulous that it was hard to pick just one. I ended up choosing two that have some colors in common to tie them together visually. Black-and-white **Chunky** creates the perfect edging.

SIZES

Instructions are written for size Small. Changes for Medium, Large, and X-Large are in parentheses. (Shown in size Small.)

FINISHED MEASUREMENTS

Across back 15½ (17¼, 19½, 20¾)"/39.5 (44, 49.5, 52.5)cm
Length 15 (16, 17½, 18)"/38 (40.5, 44.5, 45.5)cm (including ruffle)
Upper arm 12½ (14, 15¾, 16¼)"/32 (35.5, 40, 41)cm

GAUGE

15 sts and 20 rows to 4"/10cm over St st using size 10 (6mm) circular needle.
Take time to check gauge.

NOTE

Bolero is worked in one piece from the neck down.

STITCH GLOSSARY

kf&b Inc 1 by knitting into the front and back of the next st.

GARTER STITCH

Rnd 1 Purl.
Rnd 2 Knit.
Rep rnds 1 and 2 for garter st.

BOLERO

Yoke

Beg at neck edge, with shorter circular needle and A, cast on 36 (37, 39, 42) sts. Work back and forth in St st as foll:

Row 1 (RS) Knit. **Row 2** Purl. **Row 3** K2 sts (left front), pm, k7 sts (left sleeve), pm, k 18 (19, 21, 24) sts (back), pm, k7 sts (right sleeve), pm, k2 sts (right front).
Row 4 Purl across, slipping markers.
Row (inc) 5 (RS) K2, sl marker, k1, M1, *knit to 1 st before next marker, M1, k1, sl marker, k1, M1; rep from * once more, end knit to 1 st before last marker, M1, k1, sl marker, k2—42 (43, 45, 48) sts.
Row 6 Purl across, slipping markers.
Rep last 2 rows 19 (22, 25, 26) times more, end with a WS row—156 (175, 195, 204) sts. Piece should measure approx 8 (9, 10½, 11)"/20.5 (23, 26.5, 28)cm from cast-on edge of neck.

Divide for body and sleeves

Dropping markers as you go, cont to work as foll:
Next row (RS) K2 sts (left front), place next 47 (53, 59, 61) sts on holder (left sleeve), k 58 (65, 73, 78) sts (back), place next 47 (53, 59, 61) sts on holder (right sleeve), k2 sts (right front)—62 (69, 77, 82) sts. Beg with a purl row, cont in St st for 7 rows, end with a WS row.

Ruffle

Next rnd (RS) K 62 (69, 77, 82) sts, pm, pick up and k 1 st in each st and row around to bottom edge, join and pm for beg of rnds. **Next (inc) rnd** *K1, kf&b; rep from * to next marker, drop marker, then kf&b in each st to beg of rnd marker. Change to longer circular needle and B. Work around in garter st for 4"/10cm, end with rnd 1. Change to C. **Next rnd** Knit. Bind off knitwise.

Left sleeve

With RS facing, dpn, and A, k 47 (53, 59, 61) sts from left sleeve holder; divide sts evenly between 3 needles. Join and pm for beg of rnds. Work around in St st (knit every rnd) for 2"/5cm. **Dec rnd** K2tog, knit to 2 sts before marker, ssk. Rep dec rnd every 6th rnd 5 (6, 8, 8) times more—35 (39, 41, 43) sts. Work even until sleeve measures 19"/48cm from underarm. Change to C. **Next rnd** Knit. Bind off knitwise.

Right sleeve

Work as for left sleeve. ❖

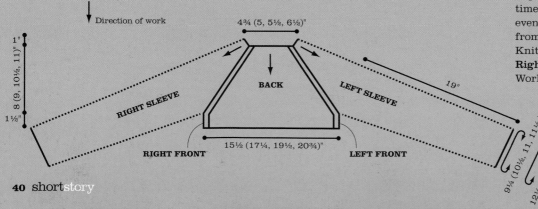

Direction of work

1"
8 (9, 10½, 11)"
1½"

4¾ (5, 5½, 6½)"

RIGHT SLEEVE

BACK

LEFT SLEEVE

19"

RIGHT FRONT

15½ (17¼, 19½, 20¾)"

LEFT FRONT

9¼ (10½, 11, 11½)"
12½ (14, 15¾, 16¼)" (upper arm)

going green

It's easy being green when you slip into this verdant
cotton and silk tweed cropped pullover.

going green

WHAT YOU NEED

Yarn
Summer Tweed **by Rowan**, 1¾oz/50g hanks, each approx 131yd/120m (silk/cotton)
• 6 (7, 8, 9) hanks in #544 jardinier

Needles
• **Two size 8 (5mm) circular needles, 29"/74cm long**, or size to obtain gauge
• **One set (5) size 8 (5mm) double-pointed needles (dpns)**

Notions
• **Stitch holders**
• **Stitch marker**

Skill Level
●●●●

SHAWL-COLLAR CROP TOP
Rowan's nubby silk and cotton **Summer Tweed** was the jumping-off point for this design. It's a beautiful fiber that requires a simple yet interesting shape to show off its intense color and texture.

SIZES
Instructions are written for size Small. Changes for Medium, Large, and X-Large are in parentheses. (Shown in size Small.)

FINISHED MEASUREMENTS
Bust 47 (51, 54, 57½)"/119.5 (129.5, 137, 146)cm
Length 11 (12, 13, 13¾)"/28 (30.5, 33, 35)cm
Upper arm 13 (14, 15, 16)"/33 (35.5, 38, 40.5)cm

GAUGES
15 sts and 20 rows to 4"/10cm over double moss st using size 8 (5mm) circular needle.
16 sts and 20 rows to 4"/10cm over St st using size 8 (5mm) circular needle.

NOTES
1) Top is worked in one piece from the neck down. **2)** Front is 2"/5cm wider than back. **3)** Fronts and back are worked in double moss st, and sleeves are worked in St st. **4)** You will be establishing pat sts on first inc row. To establish double moss st, work row 1 over left front sts, then cont pat rep over back sts, then right front sts without interruption. **5)** Work new sts into double moss st for fronts and back, and St st for sleeves as sts become available.

STITCH GLOSSARY
kf&b Inc 1 by knitting into the front and back of the next st.

DOUBLE MOSS STITCH
(over a multiple of 4 sts plus 2)

Row 1 (RS) K2, *p2, k2; rep from * to end.
Row 2 K the knit sts and p the purl sts.
Row 3 P2, *k2, p2; rep from * to end.
Row 4 K the knit sts and p the purl sts.
Rep rows 1–4 for double moss st.

K2, P2 RIB
(over a multiple of 4 sts plus 2)
Row 1 (RS) K2, *p2, k2; rep from * to end.
Row 2 P2, *k2, p2; rep from * to end.
Rep rows 1–2 for k2, p2 rib.

CROP TOP
Yoke
With circular needle, cast on 60 (62, 64, 66) sts. Working back and forth on 2 needles, cont as foll:
Next row (RS) K 2 sts (left front), pm, k 8 sts (left sleeve), pm, k 40 (42, 44, 46) sts (back), pm, k 8 sts (right sleeve), pm, k 2 sts (right front).
Next row Purl across, slipping markers.
Please see Notes 3, 4, and 5 before beg.
Inc row 1 (RS) Kf&b (left neck), *work in double moss st to 1 st before next marker (left front), kf&b, slip marker, kf&b, k to 1 st before next marker (left sleeve), kf&b, slip marker, kf&b, work in double moss st to 1 st before next marker (back), kf&b, slip marker, kf&b, k to 1 st before next marker (right sleeve), kf&b, slip marker, kf&b, work in double moss st to 1 st before last st (right front), end kf&b (right neck)—10 sts inc.
Next row Purl 1 st each side of each marker, purl sleeve sts, and work rem sts in double moss st. Rep last 2 rows 21 (20, 18, 20) times more, end with a WS row—280 (272, 254, 276) sts.

For sizes Medium, Large, and X-Large only
Inc row 1 (RS) *Work in double moss st to 1 st before next marker (left front), kf&b, slip marker, kf&b, k to 1 st before next marker (left sleeve), kf&b, slip marker, kf&b, work in double moss st to 1 st before next marker (back), kf&b, slip marker, kf&b, k to 1 st

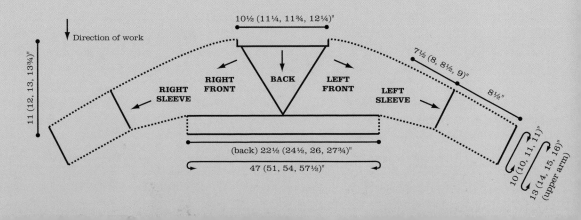

↓ Direction of work

10½ (11¼, 11¾, 12¼)"

11 (12, 13, 13¾)"

7½ (8, 8½, 9)"

8½"

RIGHT SLEEVE

RIGHT FRONT

BACK

LEFT FRONT

LEFT SLEEVE

(back) 22½ (24½, 26, 27¾)"

47 (51, 54, 57½)"

10 (10, 11, 11)"

13 (14, 15, 16)" (upper arm)

before next marker (right sleeve), kf&b, slip marker, kf&b, work in double moss st to end (right front)—8 sts inc. **Next row** Purl 1 st each side of each marker, purl sleeve sts and work rem sts in double moss st.

Inc row 3 (RS) Kf&b, *work in double moss st to 1 st before next marker (left front), kf&b, slip marker, kf&b, k to 1 st before next marker (left sleeve), kf&b, slip marker, kf&b, work in double moss st to 1 st before next marker (back), kf&b, slip marker, kf&b, k to 1 st before next marker (right sleeve), kf&b, slip marker, kf&b, work in double moss st to 1 st before last st (right front), end kf&b—10 sts inc.

Next row Purl 1 st each side of each marker, purl sleeve sts, and work rem sts in double moss st. Rep last 4 rows 1 (3, 3) time more, end with a WS row—308 (326, 348) sts.

For all sizes
Work even in pat sts as established on 280 (308, 326, 348) sts for 2 rows.

Divide for body and sleeves
Next row (RS) Work in double moss st over first 46 (50, 52, 56) sts (left front), place next 52 (58, 62, 66) sts on holder for left sleeve, work in double moss st over next 84 (92, 98, 104) sts (back), place next 52 (58, 62, 66) sts on holder for right sleeve, work in double moss st over last 46 (50, 52, 56) sts (right front)—176 (192, 202, 216) sts. Join and pm for beg of rnds. Work around in k2, p2 rib for 8 rnds. Bind off in rib.

Sleeves
With RS facing and dpn, k52 (56, 60, 64) sts from sleeve holder, dividing sts over 4 needles. Join and pm for beg of rnds. Mark last rnd. Work even in St st for 3 (3, 4, 2) rnds. **Dec rnd** K2tog, knit to last 2 sts, ssk. Rep dec rnd every 5th (3rd, 3rd, 3rd) rnd 5 (7, 7, 9) times more—40 (40, 44, 44) sts. Work even until until piece measures 7½ (8, 8½, 9)"/19 (20.5, 21.5, 23)cm above marked rnd. Cont in k2, p2 rib for 8½"/21.5cm. Bind off loosely in rib.

FINISHING
Neckband/collar
With RS facing and circular needle, pick up and k 50 (53, 56, 58) sts evenly spaced along right front neck, 10 sts across right sleeve edge, 50 (52, 54, 54) sts across back neck edge, 10 sts across left sleeve edge, then 50 (53, 56, 58) sts along left neck edge—170 (178, 186, 190) sts. Beg with row 2 (WS), cont to work back and forth in k2, p2 rib for 3½"/9cm, end with a WS row. Bind off 22 (24, 26, 26) sts at beg of next 2 rows—126 (130, 134, 138) sts. Work even for 6"/15cm. Bind off loosely in rib. Place right neckband over left neckband and sew side edges in place. ✤

tee time

Keep your cool come summer in a sporty
top knit in soft, smooth cotton.

tee time

WHAT YOU NEED

Yarn
Provence **by Classic Elite Yarns, 3½oz/100g hanks, each approx 205yd/186m (mercerized cotton)** 🔲
- **1 (1, 2, 2) hank in #2628 slate (A)**
- **2 (2, 2, 2) hanks in #2640 gunmetal grey (B)**
- **1 (1, 1, 1) hank in #2601 bleach white (C)**

Needles
- **One size 6 (4mm) circular needle, 24"/60cm long,** or size to obtain gauge

Notions
- **Stitch markers**
- **Tapestry needle**

Skill Level
●●●○

STRIPED CROPPED T-SHIRT
This fun-loving tee is a more modern, feminine take on the classic rugby shirt. A bright white neckline pops against the subdued gray stripes.

SIZES
Instructions are written for size Small. Changes for Medium, Large, and X-Large are in parentheses. (Shown in size Small.)

FINISHED MEASUREMENTS
Bust at underarm 39¾ (45¼, 49¾, 53¾)"/101 (115, 126.5, 136.5)cm
Back length 12 (13½, 15, 16¼)"/30.5 (34.5, 38, 41)cm

GAUGE
20 sts and 32 rows to 4"/10cm over St st and seed st using size 6 (4mm) needles.
Take time to check gauge.

NOTE
1) Garment is worked in one piece from the top down.
2) To make a clean line when changing colors, always make the change on a non-increase row; the change row should be either knitted (in the rnd) or purled (back and forth), disregarding the seed st pat for this change row only; resume the seed st pat for subsequent rows until you reach the next color change.
3) Schematic is on page 154.

SEED STITCH
(over a multiple of 2 sts)
Row (rnd) 1 *K1, p1; rep from * around.
Row (rnd) 2 K the purl sts and p the knit sts.
Rep row (rnd) 2 for seed st.

STRIPE SEQUENCE
*Work 24 rows (rnds) B, then 24 rows (rnds) A; rep from *.

COLLAR
Using A, cast on 52 (55, 57, 60) sts. Work back and forth.
Row 1 Knit. **Row 2** Purl.

T-SHIRT
Yoke
Row 1 (RS) K2 left front sts, pm, k1, work in seed st across 7 sleeve sts, k1, pm, k1, work in seed st across 28 (31, 33, 36) back sts, k1, pm, k1, work in seed st across 7 sleeve sts, k1, pm, k2 right front sts.
Row 2 (WS) Purl to first marker, sl marker, work in seed st across back and sleeves, slipping markers and purling 1 st either side of each marker; after last marker is slipped, purl to end.
Row (inc) 3 (RS) K to 1 st before marker, yo, k1, *sl marker, k1, yo, work in seed st to 1 st before next marker, yo, k1, sl marker; rep from * 2 times more, k1, yo, k to end—60 (63, 65, 68) sts.
Row 4 Rep row 2. **Row 5 (inc) (RS)** K1, yo, k to 1 st before first marker, yo, k1, *sl marker, k1, yo, work seed st to 1 st before next marker, yo, k1; rep from *2 times more, sl marker, k1, yo, k to 1 st before end, yo, k1—70 (73, 75, 78) sts.
Rep rows 4 and 5 11 (13, 14, 15) times more, ending with a RS row—180 (203, 215, 228) sts.
Change to B and beg stripe sequence.
Next row Purl, slipping markers.
Rep row 5 once, then rep rows 4 and 5 5 (6, 7, 8) times more, then row 4 once, ending with a WS row.
Cast on 9 (11, 12, 13) sts onto RH needle, then join and knit to first marker, which becomes the new beg marker, sl marker, and work first rnd as follows:
Rnd 1 *K1, work in seed st to 1 st before marker, k1, sl marker; rep from * twice more, k to end.
Rnd 2 (inc rnd) *K1, yo, work in seed st to 1 st before marker, yo, k1, sl marker; rep from * twice more, k1, yo, k across front to 1 st before marker, yo, k1—257 (292, 315, 339) sts.
Rep rnds 1 and 2 5 (6, 7, 8) times more, then rnd 1 once—297 (340, 371, 403) sts.
Rnd 1 K1, work in seed st across sleeve sts, k1, sl marker, k1, yo, work in seed st across back to 1 st before marker, yo, k1, sl marker, k1, work in seed st across sleeve sts, k1, sl marker, k1, yo, k across to 1 st before marker, yo, k1—301 (344, 375, 407) sts.
Rnd 2 Work around in est pats.
Rep rnds 1 and 2 4 (4, 5, 5) times more—317 (360, 395, 427) sts.
Divide yoke
Bind off 59 (67, 73, 79) left sleeve sts, work in seed st across 90 (101, 111, 120) back sts, bind off 59 (67, 73, 79) right sleeve sts, knit across 109 (125, 138, 149) front sts—199 (226, 249, 269) sts remain.
Body
Cont to work in the rnd in pats as est: Work in seed st on back sts and St st on the front sts until the current color stripe that you are working is completed.
Change color and work all sts into seed st (it may be necessary to k2tog so that seed st matches up until body measures 4¼ (5, 5¼, 6)"/11.5 (12.5, 14, 15)cm from underarm. Bind off in seed st.
Collar
Using C and with WS facing, pick up sts around neckline, join, pm, and with WS facing knit 7 rnds.
Bind off.

FINISHING
Sew together underarms.
Collar
Using C, fold collar outward and in half, covering the seam. Tack collar down on the RS by weaving the bottom stitches of the folded collar to the white loop of the picked-up row to create a clean finish. ✤

a cute angle

Take your knitting in a new direction
with this chunky ribbed poncho.

a cute angle

WHAT YOU NEED

Yarn
Burly Spun **by Brown Sheep Company,
8oz/226g hanks, each approx
132yd/121m (wool)**
• **3 (4) hanks in #BS-115 oatmeal**

Needles
• **Size 13 (9mm) circular needle,
29"/74cm long,** or size to obtain gauge

Notions
• **Stitch marker**

Skill Level
●●○○

RIBBED PONCHO

The crossover construction of this
poncho creates a striking look, and the
bold stitch pattern and folded-over
turtleneck add to the drama.

SIZES

Instructions are written for size
X-Small/Small. Changes for
Medium/Large are in parentheses.
(Shown in size X-Small/Small.)

FINISHED MEASUREMENTS

Width (at widest point) 23 (26½)"/58.5
(67.5)cm
Length of back 14 (16)"/35.5 (40.5)cm
Length of front 25½ (30)"/64.5 (76)cm

GAUGE

12 sts and 19 rows to 4"/10cm over slip
st rib using size 13 (9mm) circular
needle. **Take time to check gauge.**

NOTE

Poncho is made of one 14" x 42" (16" x
48")/35.5cm x 106.5cm (40.5cm x 122cm)
strip that is sewn to itself, leaving a neck
opening (see schematic).

SLIP STITCH RIB

(over a multiple of 4 sts plus 3)
Row 1 (RS) *K3, sl 1 wyif; rep from *,
end k3.
Row 2 K1, sl 1 wyif, *k3, sl 1 wyif; rep
from *, end k1.
Rep rows 1 and 2 for slip st rib.

PONCHO

Strip
Cast on 43 (51) sts. Work back and forth
in slip st rib until piece measures 42
(48)"/106.5 (122)cm from beg, end with a
WS row. Bind off knitwise.

FINISHING

Referring to schematic, sew bind-off edge
to RH edge of strip, forming poncho.
Neckband
With RS facing, beg at center back neck
edge and pick up and k 66 (76) sts
evenly spaced around entire neck edge.
Join and pm for beg of rnds. Work
around in k1, p1 rib for 16 rnds. Bind
off loosely in rib. Fold neckband in half
to WS and sew in place.✤

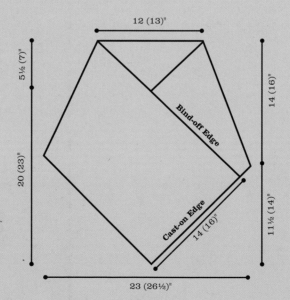

iron lady

Bobbles and a layered collar soften the edges
of this smart and sexy look.

iron lady

 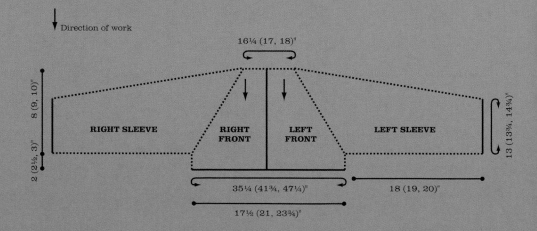
BOBBLED BOLERO
A layered collar is an easy way to create interest around the neckline, and the allover bobble-and-rib pattern adds great texture. Shorter in the back, it looks stylish worn with pants or over a dress.

SIZES
Instructions are written for size Small. Changes for Medium and Large are in parentheses. (Shown in size Small.)

FINISHED MEASUREMENTS
Back width at underarm 17½ (21, 23¾)"/44.5 (53.5, 60.5)cm
Back length 10 (11½, 13)"/ 25.5 (29, 33)cm

GAUGE
18 sts and 24 rows to 4"/10cm over yoke pat using size 9 (5.5mm) needles. **Take time to check gauge.**

NOTE
Bolero is worked from the top down.

STITCH GLOSSARY
MB (Make Bobble) Knit into the front and back loops of st until there are 6 loops on RH needle, pass the first 5 loops over the last loop, return last st to LH needle and knit it.
K1b Increase 1 st by knitting into the row below st, then knitting the st itself.

BOLERO
Collar
Wide section Using straight needles, cast on 144 (152, 160) sts. Work in garter st (knit every row) for 5"/12.5cm.
Next row K2tog-tbl across—72 (76, 80) sts. Set aside.

Narrow section Using straight needles, cast on 144 (152, 160) sts. Work in garter st for 3"/7.5cm.
Next row (WS) K2tog-tbl across—72 (76, 80) sts.
Holding the narrow section on top of the wide section, knit the 2 layers together as follows: *K the first stitch from top layer together with the first stitch from bottom layer; repeat from * across.
Next row (WS) K3, k1b, k to end—73 (77, 81) sts.
Next 3 rows Knit.
Yoke
Change to 24"/60cm circular needle and cont to work back and forth, changing to longer circular needle when necessary and slipping markers as you come to them.
Row 1 (RS) Sl 1, k2 front band sts, pm, *p1, k1; rep from * to last 4 sts, p1, pm, k3. front band sts.
Rows 2–4 Sl 1, k2, knit the k sts and purl the p sts as they appear to last 3 sts, k3.
Row 5 (inc row) (RS) Sl 1, k2, *p1, k1b; rep from * to last 4 sts, p1, k3—106 (112, 118) sts.
Row 6 (WS) Sl 1, k2, *k1, p2; rep from * to last 4 sts, k4.
Rows 7–9 Sl 1, k2, k the knit sts and p the purl sts as they appear to marker, k3.
Row 10 (inc row) (WS) Sl 1, k2, *k1b, p2; rep from * to last 4 sts, k1b, k3—140 (148, 156) sts.
Row 11 (RS) Sl 1, k2, *p2, yo, SKP; rep from * to last 5 sts, p2, k3.
Rows 12–16 Sl 1, k2, k the knit sts and p the purl sts as they appear to marker, k3.
Row 17 (inc row) (RS) Sl 1, k2, *p1, M1, p1, yo, SKP; rep from * to last 5 sts, p1, M1, p1, k3—174 (184, 194) sts.
Row 18 (WS) Sl 1, k2, *k3, p2; rep from

Direction of work

16¼ (17, 18)"

8 (9, 10)"

2 (2½, 3)"

13 (13¾, 14¾)"

RIGHT SLEEVE

RIGHT FRONT

LEFT FRONT

LEFT SLEEVE

35¼ (41¾, 47¼)"

18 (19, 20)"

17½ (21, 23¾)"

* to last 6 sts, k3, k3.

Rows 19–21 Sl 1, k2, k the knit sts and p the purl sts as they appear to marker, k3.

Row 22 (inc row) (WS) Sl 1, k2, *k3, p1, yo, p1; rep from * to last 6 sts, k3, k3—207 (219, 231) sts.

Row 23 (RS) Sl 1, k2, *p1, k1, p1, k3; rep from * to last 6 sts, p1, k1, p1, k3.

Rows 24–26 Sl 1, k2, k the knit sts and p the purl sts as they appear to marker, k3.

Row 27 (bobble row) (RS) Sl 1, k2, *p1, k1, p1, k1, MB, k1; rep from * to last 6 sts, p1, k1, p1, k3.

Row 28 (WS) Sl 1, k2, *k1, p1, k1, p3; rep from * to marker, k3.

Row 29 (inc row) (RS) Sl 1, k2, *p1, k1b, p1, k3; rep from * to last 6 sts, p1, k1b, p1, k3—241 (255, 269) sts.

Row 30 (WS) Sl 1, k2, *k1, p2, k1, p3; rep from * to last 7 sts, k1, p2, k1, k3.

Rows 31–32 Sl 1, k2, k the knit sts and p the purl sts as they appear to marker, k3.

Row 33 (bobble and inc row) (RS) Sl 1, k2, *p1, k1, yo, k1, p1, k1, MB, k1; rep from * to last 7 sts, p1, k1, yo, k1, p1, k3—275 (291, 307) sts.

Row 34 (WS) Sl 1, k2, *k1, p3; rep from * to last 8 sts, k1, p3, k1, k3.

Rows 35–38 Sl 1, k2, k the knit sts and p the purl sts as they appear to marker, k3.

Row 39 (bobble row) (RS) Sl 1, k2, *p1, k3, p1, k1, MB, k1; rep from * to last 8 sts, p1, k3, p1, k3.

Row 40 Rep row 34.

Rows 41–44 Sl 1, k2, k the knit sts and p the purl sts as they appear to marker, k3.

Row 45 Rep row 39.

Rows 46–48 Sl 1, k2, k the knit sts and p the purl sts as they appear to marker, k3.

Size Small only

Skip to yoke divide.

Sizes Medium and Large

Rows 49–51 Rep row 48.

Row 52 (inc row) (WS) Sl 1, k2, *k1b, p3, k1, p3; rep from * to last 8 sts, k1b, p3, k1, k3—(327, 345) sts.

Row 53 (bobble row) (RS) Sl 1, k2, *p1, k3, p2, k1, MB, k1; rep from * to last 9 sts, p1, k3, p2, , k3.

Row 54 Sl 1, k2, k the knit sts and p the purl sts as they appear to marker, k3.

Size Medium only

Row 55 (RS) (K19, k2tog) 15 times, end k12—312 sts.

Row 56 Knit.

Skip to yoke divide.

Size Large only

Rows 55–58 Rep row 48.

Row 59 (bobble row) (RS) Sl 1, k2, *p1, k3, p2, k1, MB, k1; rep from * to last 9 sts, p1, k3, p2, k3.

Row 60 Rep row 48.

Divide yoke

Next row (RS) Working in pats as est, work 40 (47, 53) sts for left front, place 58 (62, 66) sts on 16"/40cm circular needle and hold aside, work 79 (94, 107) sts for back, place 58 (62, 66) sts on 16"/40cm circular needle for second sleeve and hold aside, work 40 (47, 53) sts for right front—159 (188, 213) sts remain.

Work in garter st for 2 (2½, 3)"/5 (6.5, 7.6)cm. Bind off.

Sleeves

Divide 58 (62, 66) sts to 3 dpns. Working in the rnd, cont in pats as est in yoke, working bobbles every 6th rnd, and work even until sleeve measures 18 (19, 20)"/45.5 (48, 51)cm. Bind off on a bobble rnd. Repeat for second sleeve.

FINISHING

Sew body and sleeves together at underarms. Attach hook and eye to either side of upper front collar. ✣

at first blush

This casually elegant shrug only looks simple. Whisper-thin,
it's also warmer than you might think.

at first blush

CASHMERE SHRUG

Knit from one sleeve to the other in classic shrug fashion, this wrap features dropped stitches that elongate the lower half of the sleeves. It's a fun technique!

SIZES

Instructions are written for size Small. Changes for Medium, Large, and X-Large are in parentheses. (Shown in size Small.)

FINISHED MEASUREMENTS

Width across back 16 (18, 20, 22)"/40.5 (45.5, 51, 56)cm
Length of back 13½ (14¾, 16, 17¼)"/34 (37.5, 40.5, 44)cm
Upper arm 11 (12, 13, 14)"/28 (30.5, 33, 35.5)cm

GAUGE

32 sts and 36 rnds to 4"/10cm over St. John's wort st using size 3 (3.25mm) circular needle. **Take time to check gauge.**

NOTES

1) Shrug is made in one piece from left sleeve edge to right sleeve edge.
2) Sleeves are worked in the rnd and back is worked back and forth.

STITCH GLOSSARY

drop st Drop next stitch off LH needle and allow it to unravel.

ST. JOHN'S WORT STITCH

(over a multiple of 4 sts)
Rnd 1 *P2, k2; rep from * around.
Rnd 2 *P2, k1, yo, k1; rep from * around.
Rnd 3 *P2, k3; rep from * around.
Rnd 4 *P2, k3, use LH needle to pass first st over 2nd and 3rd sts just knit; rep from * around.
Rep rnds 1–4 for St. John's wort st.

SHRUG

Left sleeve
With dpn, cast on 44 (48, 52, 56) sts. Divide sts over 4 needles. Join, taking care not to twist sts on needles; pm for beg of rnds. Work around in St st (knit every rnd) for 12"/30.5cm.
Next rnd *K1, drop st; rep from * around—22 (24, 26, 28) sts.
Next rnd *K1, M1; rep from * around—44 (48, 52, 56) sts.

Next rnd Knit.
Next (inc) rnd *K1, M1; rep from * around—88 (96, 104, 112) sts.
Next rnd Knit. Cont in St. John's wort st and work even for 8"/20.5cm, end with rnd 4. Mark beg and end of last rnd for beg of back. Turn work so WS is facing.
Back
Change to circular needle. Using 2 circular needles, work back and forth in St. John's wort st (with a new multiple of 5 sts) with ribbed side borders as foll:
Row (inc) 1 (WS) [P1, k1] twice (border), *p2, k1, yo, k1; rep from * to last 4 sts, end [k1, p1] twice (border)—108 (118, 128, 138) sts.
Row 2 (RS) [K1, p1] twice, *p3, k1, yo, k1; rep from * to last 4 sts, end [p1, k1] twice.
Row 3 [P1, k1] twice, *p3, k3; rep from * to last 4 sts, end [k1, p1] twice.
Row 4 [K1, p1] twice, *p3, k3, use LH needle to pass first st over 2nd and 3rd sts just knit; rep from * to last 4 sts, end [p1, k1] twice.
Row 5 [P1, k1] twice, *p2, k3; rep from * to last 4 sts, end [k1, p1] twice. Rep rows 2–5 until piece measures 16 (18, 20, 22)"/40.5 (45.5, 51, 56)cm above marked rnd, end with row 2 (RS).
Next (dec) row [P1, k1] twice, *p3, k2tog, k1; rep from * to last 4 sts, end [k1, p1] twice—88 (96, 104, 112) sts.
Right sleeve
Change to dpns. To prevent a knot over drop st section, beg right sleeve with a new ball of yarn.
Next rnd P2, k2, *p2, k3, use LH needle to pass first st over 2nd and 3rd sts just knit; rep from * around to last 4 sts, end p2, k2. Join and pm for beg of rnds. Beg with rnd 1, cont to work around in St. John's wort st and work even for 8"/20.5cm, end with rnd 4.
Next rnd Knit.
Next (dec) rnd *K2tog; rep from * around—44 (48, 52, 56) sts.
Next rnd *K2tog, yo; rep from * around—44 (48, 52, 56) sts. Cont in St st for 12"/30.5cm.
Next rnd *K1, drop st; rep from * around—22 (24, 26, 28) sts.
Next (inc) rnd *K1, M1; rep from * around—44 (48, 52, 56) sts.
Next rnd Knit. Bind off knitwise. ❖

all tucked in

Textured tuck stitching creates exquisite detail in this pullover knit in gorgeous hand-dyed yarn.

all tucked in

WHAT YOU NEED

Yarn
Note Tanglewood Fiber Creations yarns are hand spun and hand dyed in small batches, so hank lengths will vary. Purchase yarns following yard/meter amounts.

Cashmere by Tanglewood Fiber Creations (cashmere) in calypso cove (A) (3)
- **460 (510, 565, 620)yd/420 (467, 517, 567)m; approx 1 (2, 2, 2) hanks**

Superwash Merino **by Tanglewood Fiber Creations (superwash merino) in discovery forest (B) (3)**
- **475 (525, 578, 636)yd/435 (480, 529, 582)m; approx 1 (2, 2, 2) hanks**

Needles
- **Two size 7 (4.5mm) circular needles, 29"/74cm long,** or size to obtain gauge
- **Size 7 (4.5mm) circular needle, 16"/40cm long**
- **One set (5) size 7 (4.5mm) double-pointed needles (dpns)**

Notions
- **Stitch holders**
- **Stitch marker**
- **2yd/2m contrasting cotton crochet thread**
- **Tapestry needle**

Skill Level
●●●○

TUCKED-HEM CROP TOP
Several years ago, I designed a tea cozy using tucking, a form of knitted pleating, and loved the results. I "tucked" the idea in the back of my mind to use in a garment one day. Tucking takes time, patience, and good lighting, but it's well worth the effort.

SIZES
Instructions are written for size Small. Changes for Medium, Large, and X-Large are in parentheses. (Shown in size Small.)

FINISHED MEASUREMENTS
Bust 36 (40, 44, 48)"/91.5 (101.5, 111.5, 122)cm
Length 13½ (14, 14½, 15)"/34 (35.5, 37, 38)cm

Upper arm 13 (14, 15, 16)"/33 (35.5, 38, 40.5)cm

GAUGE
21 sts and 28 rnds to 4"/10cm over St st using size 7 (4.5mm) circular needle. **Take time to check gauge.**

NOTES
1) Top is worked in one piece from the neckband down.
2) Yoke and sleeves are worked in St st with a purl ridge on the WS. When piece is turned to RS, RS is now reverse St st with a knit ridge.
3) Tucking rnds are worked in St st, with the RS facing.
4) Schematic is on page 155.

STITCH GLOSSARY
kf&b Inc 1 by knitting into the front and back of the next st.

TOP

Neckband
With shorter circular needle and A, cast on 90 (94, 100, 106) sts. Join, taking care not to twist sts on needle, pm for beg of rnds.
Rnds 1–16 (WS) Knit.

Yoke
Cont to work with WS facing as foll:
Rnd (inc) 1 *K1, kf&b; rep from * around—135 (141, 150, 159) sts.
Rnd (ridge) 2 Purl. (Mark last rnd only.)
Rnds 3–9 Knit. Change to longer circular needle.
Rnd (inc) 10 *K2, kf&b; rep from * around—180 (188, 200, 212) sts.
Rnds 11–17 Rep rnds 2–9.
Rnd (inc) 18 *K3, kf&b; rep from * around—225 (235, 250, 265) sts.
Rnds 19–25 Rep rnds 2–9.
Rnd (inc) 26 *K4, kf&b; rep from * around—270 (282, 300, 318) sts.
Rnds 27–33 Rep rnds 2–9.
Rnd (inc) 34 *K5, kf&b; rep from * around—315 (329, 350, 371) sts.
Rnds 35–41 Rep rnds 2–9.
Rnd (inc) 42 *K104 (14, 10, 8), kf&b; rep from * around, end k 0 (14, 20, 2)—318 (350, 380, 412) sts.
Rnds 43–49 Rep rnds 2–9.
Rnd 50 Knit.
Rnd 51 Purl. Cont in St st (knit every rnd), work even until piece measures 8 (8½, 9, 9½)"/20.5 (21.5, 23, 24)cm above marked rnd.

Dividing for body and sleeves
Cont to work with WS facing as foll:
Next rnd K 93 (103, 114, 124) front sts, cast on 2 sts for underarm, place next 66 (72, 76, 82) sts on holder for sleeve, k 93 (103, 114, 124) back sts, cast on 2 sts for underarm, place rem 66 (72, 76, 82) on holder for sleeve—190 (210, 232, 252) sts. Join and pm for beg of rnds.

Body
Cont to work with WS facing as foll:
Next 7 rnds Knit.

Tucking
Turn work so RS (reverse St st) is facing. Thread crochet cotton into tapestry needle. Change to B. With RS facing, cont to work as foll:
Rnds 1 and 2 (RS) Knit.
Rnd (marking) 3 *K10, working from right to left, insert tapestry needle through sts just knitted on RH needle; rep from * around, end last rep k 10 (10, 12, 12), working from right to left, insert tapestry needle through sts on RH needle.
Rnds 4–14 Knit.
Rnd (tuck) 15 With WS (purl side) facing, and beg with first st of marked rnd, use 2nd circular needle to pick up each st around. Pull out crochet cotton in one length so it can be used again. With WS tog and LH needles parallel, insert a dpn knitwise into first st of each needle and wrap yarn around each needle as if to knit. Knit these 2 sts tog and sl them off the needles. *K the next 2 sts tog in the same manner; rep from * around—tuck made.
Rnds 16–18 Knit. **Rnd (marking) 19** Rep rnd 3. **Rnds 20–30** Knit.
Rnd (tuck) 31 Rep rnd 15. Rep rnds 16–31 twice more, then rnds 16–30 once.
Last rnd Rep rnd 31, binding off knitwise as you go.

Sleeves
With WS facing, dpn, and A, p 66 (72, 76, 82) sts from sleeve holder, then cast on 2 sts for underarm—68 (74, 78, 84) sts. Divide sts over 4 needles. Join, taking care not to twist sts on needles; pm for beg of rnds.
Rnd (ridge) 1 Purl.
Rnds 2–17 Knit. Bind off loosely knitwise.

FINISHING
Sew underarm sts tog. Fold neckband to WS along first purl ridge and sew in place. Fold sleeves to WS along purl ridge and sew in place. ❖

hyacinth bouclé

Fabulously frothy bouclé yarn takes a simple
shape and makes it simply irresistible.

hyacinth bouclé

WHAT YOU NEED

Yarn
Loopy **by Tilli Tomas, 1¾oz/50g skeins, each approx 55yd/50m (kid mohair/wool/nylon) (5)**
• **8 (9, 10, 11) skeins in #15 eternal diva**

Needles
• **One each size 10 (6mm) circular needles, 29"/74cm long and 24"/60cm long,** or size to obtain gauge
• **Two size 10 (6mm) circular needles, 16"/40cm long**
• **Set of (4) size 10 (6mm) double-pointed needles (dpns)**

Notions
• **Stitch markers**
• **Tapestry needle**
• **One hook and eye set (⅜"/1cm)**

Skill Level
●●●○

BOUCLÉ BOLERO

For me, a great bouclé yarn is hard to resist. It's luxurious and brimming with texture and luminosity. I kept this bolero simple to showcase the yarn, but added a front faux-tie detail for a bit of flair.

SIZES

Instructions are written for size Small. Changes for Medium, Large, and X-Large are in parentheses. (Shown in size Small.)

FINISHED MEASUREMENTS

Back at underarm 17¼ (18¾, 20¾, 22)"/44 (47.5, 52.5, 56)cm
Back length 11¾ (12½, 14¼, 15)"/30 (31.5, 36, 38)cm

GAUGES

12 sts and 22 rows (rnds) to 4"/10cm over garter st using size 10 (6mm) needles.
12 sts and 14 rows (rnds) to 4"/10cm over St st using size 10 (6mm) needles. **Take time to check gauges.**

NOTE

Bolero is worked in one piece from the top down.

STITCH GLOSSARY

Kf&b Inc 1 by knitting into the front and back of the next st.

BOLERO

Collar
Using 24"/60cm circular needle, cast on 72 (75, 81, 84) sts. Work back and forth in garter st (knit every row) for 5 (5, 6, 6)"/12.5 (12.5, 15, 15)cm.
Next row *K1, k2tog; rep from * across—48 (50, 54, 56) sts.

Yoke
Row 1 (RS) K10 (11, 12, 13) left front sts, pm, k6 sleeve sts, pm, k 16 (16, 18, 18) back sts, pm, k6 sleeve sts, pm, k 10 (11, 12, 13) right front sts.
Row 2 (WS) K across, slipping markers.
Row 3 (inc) (RS) *K to 1 st before next marker, kf&b, sl marker, kf&b; rep from * 3 times more, k to end—56 (58, 62, 64) sts. Rep last 2 rows 17 (19, 21, 23) times more, then row 2 once, ending with a WS row—192 (210, 230, 248) sts.
Divide yoke
Row 1 (RS) K 28 (31, 34, 37) left front sts, pm, place 42 (46, 50, 54), sleeve sts onto a 16"/40cm circular needle and hold aside, k 52 (56, 62, 66) back sts, pm, place 42 (46, 50, 54) sleeve sts onto a 16"/40cm circular needle and hold aside, k 28 (31, 34, 37) right front sts—108 (118, 130, 140) sts remain.
Body
Rows 2–6 Cont to work in garter st.
Row 7 (RS) *K to 2 sts before first underarm marker, k2tog-tbl, sl marker, k2tog; rep from * once more for second underarm marker, k to end—104 (114, 126, 136) sts. **Row 8–12** Knit.
Rep rows 7–12 2 times more—96 (106, 118, 128) sts. Work in garter st until body measures 5 (5, 6, 6)"/12.5 (12.5, 15, 15)cm from underarm.
Next row K2tog to first underarm marker, remove marker, k across back to next underarm marker, remove marker, k2tog to end. Bind off.
Sleeves
Return to 42 (46, 50, 54) held sleeve sts. Work St st (k every rnd) in the rnd for 10 (11, 12, 12)"/25.5 (28, 30.5, 30.5)cm.
Next rnd *K1, k2tog; rep from * around, end k 0 (1, 2, 0)—28 (32, 36, 36) sts. Knit 2 rnds. Bind off. Rep for 2nd sleeve.

FRONT SCARF PIECES (make 2)

Using dpns, cast on 18 sts; working back and forth, work in garter st until piece measures 7 (7, 8, 8)"/18 (18, 20, 20)cm long.
Next row K2tog across—9 sts.
Next row K2tog across, end k1—5 sts. Bind off.

FINISHING

Sew body and sleeves tog at underarm. Sew narrow end of scarf pieces to top of each sweater front just under collar. Attach hook and eye at top of sweater front just under collar. ❖

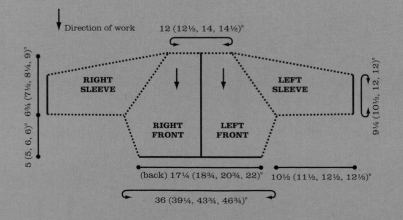

↓ Direction of work

12 (12½, 14, 14½)"

5 (5, 6, 6)" 6¾ (7½, 8¼, 9)"

RIGHT SLEEVE

LEFT SLEEVE

RIGHT FRONT

LEFT FRONT

9¼ (10½, 12, 12)"

(back) 17¼ (18¾, 20¾, 22)" 10½ (11½, 12½, 12½)"

36 (39¼, 43¾, 46¾)"

block party

Bulky knit squares framed by an oversized collar create
a cropped bolero that is larger than life.

block party

WHAT YOU NEED

Yarn
Soft Chunky **by Twinkle Handknits/ Classic Elite Yarns, 7oz/200g hanks, each approx 83yd/76m (virgin wool)** 🌀
• 5 (6) hanks in #54 quartz (A)
• 4 (5) hanks in #18 french grey (B)

Needles
• **One set (5) size 17 (12.75mm) double-pointed needles (dpns),** or size to obtain gauge
• **Size 13 (9mm) circular needle, 29"/74cm long**

Notions
• **Stitch marker**

Skill Level
●●●○

PATCHWORK BOLERO

Here's a new take on the traditional granny square. Grannies are usually crocheted, but here I knit them in a bulky yarn. Using just two colors restrains the extroverted design, but you could raid your bulky stash to work it in a more exuberant palette.

SIZES

Instructions are written for size Small/Medium. Changes for Large/ X-Large are in parentheses. (Shown in size Small/Medium.)

FINISHED MEASUREMENTS

Bust 45 (63)"/114.5 (160)cm
Length 13½"/34cm
Upper arm 18"/45.5cm

GAUGE

One motif to 4½" x 4½"/11.5cm x 11.5cm using size 17 (12.75mm) dpns. **Take time to check gauge.**

NOTE

Assembly diagram for size Large/X-Large is on page 155.

K2, P2 RIB

(over a multiple of 4 sts plus 2)
Row 1 (RS) K2, *p2, k2; rep from * to end.
Row 2 P2, *k2, p2; rep from * to end.
Rep rows 1 and 2 for k2, p2 rib.

MOTIF

With dpn and A, cast on 12 sts. Divide sts over 4 needles. Join, taking care not to twist sts on needles; pm for beg of rnds.
Rnd 1 Knit.
Rnd 2 *K1, M1, k1, M1, k1; rep from * around 3 times more—20 sts.
Rnd 3 Knit.
Rnd 4 *K1, M1, k3, M1, k1; rep from * around 3 times more—28 sts.
Rnd 5 Knit.
Rnd 6 *K1, M1, k5, M1, k1; rep from * around 3 times more—36 sts. Bind off knitwise. Make 21 (26) more using A, then 21 (28) using B.

FINISHING

Lightly block motifs 4½"/11.5cm square. Working through back lps, whipstitch motifs tog foll assembly diagram.
Collar
With WS facing, circular needle, and A, pick up and k 30 sts evenly spaced along left front edge, 10 sts along back neck edge, then 30 sts along right front edge—70 sts. Beg with row 2, cont in k2, p2 rib for 13 (15) rows, end with a WS row. Change to B.
Next row (RS) Knit. Beg with row 2, cont in k2, p2 rib for 13 (15) rows, end with a WS row. Bind off loosely in rib. Whipstitch side and sleeve seams. ❧

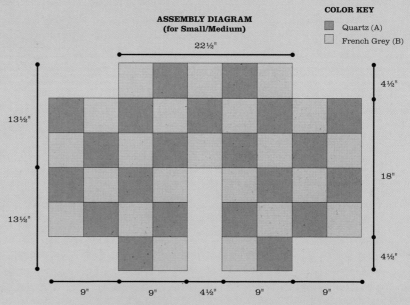

ASSEMBLY DIAGRAM
(for Small/Medium)

COLOR KEY
■ Quartz (A)
□ French Grey (B)

22½"

4½"

13½"

18"

13½"

4½"

9"   9"   4½"   9"   9"

(Assembly diagram for Large/X-Large is on page 155.)

spring fling

Organic cotton in quiet shades of cream and pale gray creates the perfect top to slip into when the weather warms up.

spring fling

TWO-TONE PULLOVER
I love how the ribbed fabric of this light topper gently hugs the shoulders. It's feminine and charming and as effortless to make as it is to wear.

SIZES
Instructions are written for size Small. Changes for Medium, Large, and X-Large are in parentheses. (Shown in size Small.)

FINISHED MEASUREMENTS
Bust 50½ (53½, 56, 58½)"/128 (136, 142, 148.5)cm
Length 12 (13, 14, 15)"/30.5 (33, 35.5, 38)cm

GAUGE
18 sts and 29 rnds to 4"/10cm over broken rib using size 7 (4.5mm) circular needle. **Take time to check gauge.**

NOTES
1) Body is worked in the rnd to armholes.
2) Back and front bodices and yoke are worked back and forth.

STITCH GLOSSARY
K inc (knit increase) Knit next st in the row below, then knit same st in the working row.

BROKEN RIB
(over a multiple of 2 sts; worked in the rnd)
Rnd 1 Knit.
Rnd 2 *K1, p1; rep from * around.
Rep rnds 1 and 2 for broken rib.

BROKEN RIB
(over a multiple of 2 sts; worked back and forth)
Row 1 (RS) Knit.
Row 2 *K1, p1; rep from * to end.
Rep rows 1 and 2 for broken rib.

K2, P2 RIB
(over a multiple of 4 sts plus 2)
Row 1 (RS) K2, *p2, k2; rep from * to end.
Row 2 P2, *k2, p2; rep from * to end.
Rep rows 1 and 2 for k2, p2 rib.

BODY
With MC, cast on 180 (192, 204, 216) sts. Join and pm for beg of rnds.
Next rnd K 90 (96, 102, 108), pm (side marker), knit to end. Beg with rnd 2, cont to work in the rnd in broken rib until piece measures 4 (4½, 5, 5½)"/10 (11.5, 12.5, 14)cm from beg, end with rnd 2.

Side shaping
Next (inc) rnd K inc, knit to 1 st before side marker, K inc, sl marker, K inc, knit to 1 st before rnd marker, K inc—184 (196, 208, 220) sts.
Next rnd *K1, p1; rep from * around. Rep last 2 rnds 11 times more—228 (240, 252, 264) sts.

Back bodice
Next row (RS) Using 2nd circular needle, k 114 (120, 126, 132) sts; leave rem 114 (120, 126, 132) sts on first needle for front bodice. Beg with row 2, cont to work back and forth in broken rib using 2 needles for 2½ (3, 3½, 4)"/6.5 (7.5, 9, 10)cm, end with a WS row. Leave sts on needle.

Front bodice
Next row (RS) Beg with row 1, cont to work back and forth in broken rib using 2 needles for 2½ (3, 3½, 4)"/6.5 (7.5, 9, 10)cm, end with a WS row.

Front yoke
Change to CC.
Next row (RS) With CC, knit across, inc 0 (2, 0, 2) sts evenly spaced—114 (122, 126, 134) sts.
Next row (WS) [P2,k2] 9 (10, 10, 11) times, p 42 (42, 46, 46), [k2, p2] 9 (10, 10, 11) times.
Next row [K2, p2] 9 (10, 10, 11) times, k 42 (42, 46, 46), [p2, k2] 9 (10, 10, 11) times. Rep last 2 rows for 3"/7.5cm, end a WS row.

Neck opening
Next row (RS) [K2, p2] 9 (10, 10, 11) times, bind off center 42 (42, 46, 46) sts, [p2, k2] 9 (10, 10, 11) times.
Next row [P2,k2] 9 (10, 10, 11) times, cast on 42 (42, 46, 46) sts, [k2, p2] 9 (10, 10, 11) times.
Next row K2, *p2, k2; rep from * to end. Beg with row 2, cont in k2, p2 rib until back yoke measures 3"/7.5cm from cast-on edge of neck opening, end with a WS row.

FINISHING
Join bottom edge of back yoke to top edge of back bodice using 3-needle bind-off. ❧

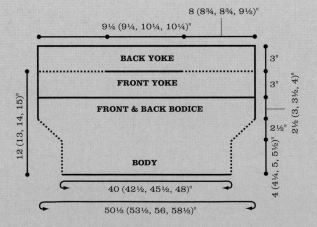

short 'n' sweet

This delectable confection spun from cashmere and silk will satisfy any sweet tooth.

short 'n' sweet

COWLNECK CAPELET

This cashmere-and-silk yarn is hand spun and hand dyed, resulting in a fiber that is truly one of a kind. I kept the design simple to not compete with the interesting yarn, but then tossed in a few structural twists. The neckline is worked back and forth, gradually adding stitches to create a plunging cowl neck; two stitch patterns provide texture.

SIZES

Instructions are written for size Small. Changes for Medium, Large, and X-Large are in parentheses. (Shown in size Small.)

FINISHED MEASUREMENTS

Bottom circumference 43½ (45¼, 47, 49)"/110.5 (115.5, 119.5, 124.5)cm
Length 16 (16½, 17, 17½)"/40.5 (42, 43, 44.5)cm (excluding collar)

GAUGE

22 sts and 24 rows to 4"/10cm over simple diagonal relief stitch using size 8 (5mm) circular needle. **Take time to check gauge.**

NOTES

1) Each hank of this handmade art yarn varies in tonality. To prevent obvious color changes, work with 2 hanks of yarn throughout. When working back and forth, change from one hank to the other every RS row. When working in the round, change from one hank to the other every other rnd.
2) Capelet is worked in one piece from the neck down.

STITCH GLOSSARY

K inc (knit increase) Knit next st in the row below, then knit same st on the working row.

SIMPLE DIAGONAL RELIEF STITCH

(over a multiple of 4 sts)
Rnd 1 *P2, k2; rep from * around.
Rnd 2 *K1, p2, k1; rep from * around.
Rnd 3 *K2, p2; rep from * around.
Rnd 4 *P1, k2, p1; rep from * around.
Rep rnds 1–4 for simple diagonal relief st.

CAPELET

Beg at back neck edge, cast on 44 (46, 48, 50) sts. Work back and forth as foll:
Rows 1–6 *K1, p1; rep from * to end.

Row (inc) 7 (RS) *K inc, p1; rep from * to end—66 (69, 72, 75) sts.
Row 8 *K1, p2; rep from * to end.
Rows 9–13 K the knit sts and p the purl sts.
Row (inc) 14 (WS) *K inc, p2; rep from * to end—88 (92, 96, 100) sts.
Row 15 *K2, p2; rep from * to end.
Rows 16–20 K the knit sts and p the purl sts.
Row (inc) 21 (RS) *K1, M1, k1, p2; rep from * to end—110 (115, 120, 125) sts.
Row 22 *K2, p3; rep from * to end.
Rows 23–27 K the knit sts and p the purl sts.
Row (inc) 28 (WS) *K1, M1, k1, p3; rep from * to end—132 (138, 144, 150) sts.
Row 29 *K3, p3; rep from * to end.
Rows 30–34 K the knit sts and p the purl sts.
Row (inc) 35 (RS) *K1, K inc, k1, p3; rep from * to end—154 (161, 168, 175) sts.
Row 36 *K3, p4; rep from * to end.
Rows 37–41 K the knit sts and p the purl sts.
Row (inc) 42 (WS) *K1, K inc, k1, p4; rep from * to end—176 (184, 192, 200) sts.
Row 43 *K4, p4; rep from * to end.
Rows 44–54 K the knit sts and p the purl sts.
Row (inc) 55 (RS) *K2, M1, k2, p4; rep from * to end—198 (207, 216, 225) sts.
Row 56 *K4, p5; rep from * to end.
Rows 57–65 K the knit sts and p the purl sts.
Row (inc) 66 (WS) *K2, M1, k2, p5; rep from * to end, then cast on 20 sts—240 (250, 260, 270) sts. Join and pm for beg of rnds. Cont to work around as foll:
Rnds 1–10 *K5, p5; rep from * around.
Rnd 11 *K2, p1, k2, p2, k1, p2; rep from * around. Rep rnd 11 until piece measures 16 (16¼, 17, 17½)"/40.5 (42, 43, 44.5)cm from neck edge. Bind off loosely in rib pat.

Collar

With RS facing, pick up and k 44 (46, 48, 50) sts along back neck edge, 58 (57, 58, 57) sts evenly spaced along left neck edge, 20 sts along front neck edge, then 58 (57, 58, 57) sts evenly spaced along right neck edge—180 (180, 184, 184) sts. Join and pm for beg of rnds. Work around in simple diagonal relief st for approx 5"/12.5cm), end with rnd 4.
Next (eyelet) rnd *P2, k2tog, yo; rep from * around. Cont with rnd 2, work in simple diagonal relief st for 4"/10cm more. Bind off loosely in pat st.

FINISHING

Beg and ending at center front, weave leather cording through eyelets. ❖

belle curve

The unusual construction of this lovely cardi creates
an arched front and a gently curved back.

belle curve

WHAT YOU NEED

Yarn
Lamb's Pride Superwash Worsted **by Brown Sheep Company, 3½oz/100g balls, each approx 200yd/183m (superwash wool)**
• 4 (5, 6, 6) balls in #SW57 cornflower

Needles
• **Two size 8 (5mm) circular needles, 24"/60cm long,** or size to obtain gauge
• **One set (5) size 8 (5mm) double-pointed needles (dpns)**

Notions
• **Stitch holders**
• **Stitch marker**
• **Three 1"/25mm buttons**

Skill Level
●●●●

BUTTON-FRONT CARDI

This design is an interesting variation on a classic top-down cardigan. Changing the yoke increases so that the front is a constant width creates a horizontal plane as the sleeves and back are knitted and shaped. It's a new shape that will keep the most curious wondering how you did it.

SIZES

Instructions are written for size Small. Changes for Medium, Large, and X-Large are in parentheses. (Shown in size Small.)

FINISHED MEASUREMENTS

Bust (closed) 40 (45, 46½, 51½)"/101.5 (114.5, 118, 131)cm
Length 16 (17¼, 19, 20½)"/40.5 (44, 48, 52)cm
Upper arm 11½ (12½, 13½, 14½)"/29 (32, 34, 37)cm

GAUGE

24 sts and 24 rows to 4"/10cm over k1, p1 rib using size 8 (5mm) circular needle (unstretched). **Take time to check gauge.**

NOTES

1) Cardi is worked in one piece from the neckband down.
2) Schematic shows cardi lying flat and does not represent how it fits on the body when buttoned.

K1, P1 RIB

(over a multiple of 2 sts plus 1)
Row 1 (RS) K1, *p1, k1; rep from * to end.
Row 2 P1, *k1, p1; rep from * to end.
Rep rows 1 and 2 for k1, p1 rib.

CARDI

Neckband
With circular needle, cast on 139 (149, 155, 165) sts. Working back and forth using 2 circular needles, work even in k1, p1 rib for 4 rows.

Yoke
Next row (RS) Work in rib over first 41 (45, 47, 51) sts (left front), pm, k2, work in rib over next 25 (26, 27, 28) sts (left back), k1, pm (center back marker), k2, work in rib over next 25 (26, 27, 28) sts (right back), k2, pm, work in rib over last 41 (45, 47, 51) sts (right front).
Next (buttonhole) row (WS) Slipping markers as you go, work in rib over first 6 sts, bind off next 3 sts, [work in rib over next 9 (11, 13, 15) sts, bind off next 3 sts] twice, work in rib to end.
Inc row 1 (RS) Casting on 3 sts over bound-off sts, work in rib to first marker, slip marker, [k1, M1] twice, work in rib to 1 st before center back marker, work (M1, k1, M1), slip marker, [k1, M1] twice, work in rib to 2 sts before last marker, [M1, k1] twice, slip marker, work in rib to end—147 (157, 163, 173) sts.
Next row Work in rib to marker, slip marker, p2, work in rib to 2 sts before center back marker, p2, slip marker, p1, work in rib to 2 sts before last marker, p2, slip marker, work in rib to end.

Inc row 2 (RS) Work in rib to first marker, slip marker, [k1, M1] twice, work in rib to 1 st before center back marker, work (M1, k1, M1), slip marker, [k1, M1] twice, work in rib to 2 sts before last marker, [M1, k1] twice, slip marker, work in rib to end.
Next row Work in rib to marker, slip marker, p2, work in rib to 2 sts before center back marker, p2, slip marker, p1, work in rib to 2 sts before last marker, p2, slip marker, work in rib to end. Rep last 2 rows 28 (32, 37, 41) times more, end with a WS row—379 (421, 467, 509) sts.
Divide for body and sleeves
Dec row 1 (RS) Work in rib over first 41 (45, 47, 51) sts (left front), place next 70 (76, 82, 88) sts on holder for left sleeve, work in rib to 2 sts before center back marker, SKP, slip marker, k1, k2tog, work in rib over next 70 (76, 82, 88) sts before last marker, place 70 (76, 82, 88) sts on holder for right sleeve, work in rib over last 41 (45, 47, 51) sts (right front)—237 (267, 301, 331) sts.
Next row Work in rib pat as established.
Dec row 2 (RS) Work in rib to 2 sts before center back marker, SKP, slip marker, k1, k2tog, work in rib to end. Rep last 2 rows twice more, end with a RS row. Bind off in rib, dec 1 st each side of center back marker as established
Sleeves
With RS facing and dpn, work in rib over 70 (76, 82, 88) sts from sleeve holder, dividing sts over 4 needles. Join and pm for beg of rnds. Work around in rib for 9 (9, 9½, 10)"/23 (23, 24, 25.5)cm. Bind off in rib.

FINISHING

Sew on buttons with yarn. Knot in front of button, leaving a short tail. ✤

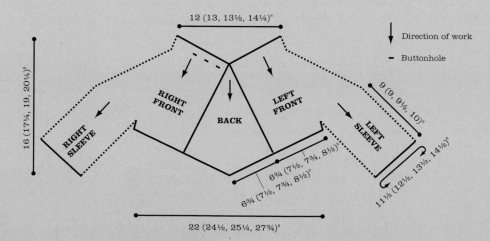

12 (13, 13½, 14¼)"
16 (17¼, 19, 20½)"
RIGHT FRONT
LEFT FRONT
BACK
RIGHT SLEEVE
LEFT SLEEVE
9 (9, 9½, 10)"
6¾ (7½, 7¾, 8½)"
6¾ (7½, 7¾, 8½)"
11½ (12½, 13½, 14½)"
22 (24½, 25¼, 27¾)"

→ Direction of work
– Buttonhole

in the pink

Knit in vivid candy pink merino with a decadent layered collar,
this fetching bolero gives off a rosy glow.

in the pink

WHAT YOU NEED

Yarn
Worsted Merino **by Catskill Merino,**
1¾oz/50g skeins, each approx 140yd/127.5m
(merino wool)
• 6 (7, 7, 8) skeins in #1 deep cochineal

Needles
• **Three size 9 (5.5mm) circular needles,**
24"/60cm long, or size to obtain gauge
• **Two size 9 (5.5mm) circular needles,**
16"/40cm long
• **Set of (4) size 9 (5.5mm) double-pointed**
needles (dpns)

Notions
• **One 1"/25mm button**
• **Stitch markers**
• **Tapestry needle**

Skill Level
●●●●

BASKETWEAVE BOLERO

Late one afternoon, as I was walking
through the Union Square Greenmarket
in New York, my eyes locked onto a stand
brimming with gorgeous yarns spun from
local wool. Several months later, Eugene
Wyatt, the owner of Catskill Merino, sent
me some of this fabulous yarn to play
with. It's super lightweight and lofty and
comes in an array of exquisite colors.

SIZES

Instructions are written for size Small.
Changes for Medium, Large, and X-Large
are in parentheses. (Shown in size Small.)

FINISHED MEASUREMENTS

Back width at underarm 18 (20, 22,
24)"/45.5 (51, 56, 61)cm
Back length 10¾ (11¾, 13¾, 14½)"/27.5
(30, 35, 37)cm

GAUGE

16 sts and 24 rows (rnds) to 4"/10cm over
checkerboard st using size 9 (5.5mm)
needle. **Take time to check gauge.**

NOTE

Bolero is worked in one piece from the
top down.

CHECKERBOARD STITCH

(over a multiple of 10 sts, worked back
and forth)
Rows 1–6 *K5, p5; rep from * across.
Rows 7–12 *P5, k5; rep from * across.
Rep rows 1–12 for checkerboard stitch.

CHECKERBOARD STITCH

(over a multiple of 10 sts, worked in the rnd)
Rnds 1–6 *K5, p5; rep from * around.
Rnds 7–12 *P5, k5; rep from * around.
Rep rnds 1–12 for checkerboard stitch.

K1, P1 RIB

(over a multiple of 2 sts, worked back
and forth)
Row 1 *K1, p1; rep from * across.
Row 2 K the knit sts and p the purl sts.
Rep row 2 for k1, p1 rib.

BOLERO

Collar
Layer #1
Using 24"/60cm circular needle, cast on
128 (136, 144, 152) sts. Working back
and forth, work k1, p1 rib until piece
measures 3½"/9cm.
Next row K2tog-tbl across—64 (68, 72,
76) sts. Set aside.
Layer #2
Using second 24"/60cm circular needle,
cast on 128 (136, 144, 152) sts. Working
back and forth, work k1, p1 rib until
piece measures 2½"/6.5cm.
Next row K2tog-tbl across—64 (68, 72,
76) sts.
Assemble collar: step 1
With layer #2 on top of layer #1, knit the
two collars together using the third
24"/60cm circular needle.
Next row (WS) Purl. Hold aside.
Layer #3
Using 24"/60cm circular needle, cast on
128 (136, 144, 152) sts. Working back
and forth, work k1, p1 rib until piece
measures 1½"/4cm.
Next row K2tog-tbl across—64 (68, 72,
76) sts.
Assemble collar: step 2
With layer #3 on top of the assembled collar
(#2 and #1), knit the two pieces together
using the third 24"/60cm circular needle.
Cast on 5 sts (front border) at the end.
Next row (WS) Knit across. Cast on 5 sts
(front border) at the end. Knit 4 rows.
Next (buttonhole) row (RS) K3, bind off
2 sts, k across.
Next row (WS) Knit, casting on 2 sts
over bound-off sts in the previous row.
Knit 2 rows.

YOKE

Note RS is now the opposite side of the
layered collar.
Row 1 (WS) K 19 (20, 21, 22) right front
sts, pm, k 8 sleeve sts, pm, k 20 (22, 24,
26) back sts, pm, k 8 sleeve sts, pm, k 19
(20, 21, 22) left front sts.
Row (inc) 2 (RS) Work checkerboard pat
to 1 st before marker, yo, k1, sl marker

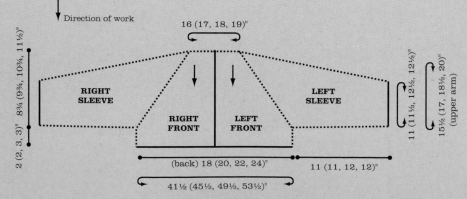

Direction of work

16 (17, 18, 19)"

8¾ (9¾, 10¾, 11½)"

2 (2, 3, 3)"

**RIGHT
SLEEVE**

**RIGHT
FRONT**

**LEFT
FRONT**

**LEFT
SLEEVE**

11 (11½, 12¾, 12½)"

15½ (17, 18½, 20)"
(upper arm)

(back) 18 (20, 22, 24)"

11 (11, 12, 12)"

41½ (45½, 49½, 53½)"

(slm), k1, yo; rep from * 3 times more (work checkerboard pat to end, but make sure to establish the pat so that it works out to an even 5 sts at the front border, by counting back from the front edge to where you are and then working forward)—82 (86, 90, 94) sts.

Row 3 (WS) Work increases into checkerboard pat as established for each section and keep 1 st either side of each marker in St st (k on RS, p on WS). Rep last 2 rows 25 (28, 31, 34) times more, ending with a WS row—282 (310, 338, 366) sts.

Divide yoke
Work est checkerboard pat across 45 (49, 53, 57) left front sts, cast on 2 sts at underarm and pm between them, place 60 (66, 72, 78) sleeve sts onto a 16"/40cm circular needle and hold aside, work est checkerboard across 72 (80, 88, 96) back sts, cast on 2 sts at underarm and pm between them, place 60 (66, 72, 78) sleeve sts onto a 16"/40cm circular needle and hold aside, work across in est checkerboard pat 45 (49, 53, 57) right front sts—166 (182, 198, 214) sts remain.

BODY
Work back and forth in the est checkerboard pat until 2 (2, 3, 3) squares of the checkerboard pat have been worked vertically—approx 2 (2, 3, 3)"/5 (5, 7.5, 7.5)cm. (**Note** Patterns at underarms may not "match up"; keep to pats as established for back and fronts.) Bind off.

SLEEVES
Divide 60 (66, 72, 78) sleeve sts onto 3 dpns, cast on 2 sts at underarm and pm between them, and join to beg working in the rnd—62 (68, 74, 80) sts.
Work in est checkerboard pat for 1"/2.5cm.
Next (dec) rnd K2tog, work around in est pat, end k2tog—60 (66, 72, 78) sts.
Work 5 (4, 4, 3) rnds in pat.
Rep last 6 (5, 5, 4) rnds 8 (10, 11, 14) times more—44 (46, 50, 50) sts.
Work another 1"/2.5cm in pat, end on rnd 6 or 12. Bind off loosely.
Rep for second sleeve.

FINISHING
Sew body and sleeves together at underarm. Attach button to left-hand side of top sweater front. ✤

high contrast

A striking black-and-white color scheme, deeply textured stitch pattern, and simple but bold shape are the height of fashion.

high contrast

WHAT YOU NEED

Yarn
Chunky **by Misti Alpaca,**
3½oz/100g hanks, each approx
109yd/100m (baby alpaca)
• **4 (5) hanks in #2L470 black/cream**

Needles
• **Size 10 (6mm) circular needles,**
16"/40cm and 29"/74cm long, or size to
obtain gauge

Notions
• **Stitch marker**

Skill Level
●●○○

BRIOCHE-STITCH PONCHO

The ribbing in this design hugs the body
to keep out the chill. Simple or minimal
designs like this are good candidates for
highly textured and dramatically colored
yarns, and you can't go wrong with
classic black and white.

SIZES

Instructions are written for size
Small/Medium. Changes for Large/
X-Large are in parentheses. (Shown in
size Small/Medium.)

FINISHED MEASUREMENTS

Bottom circumference (unstretched) 35
(40)"/89 (101.5)cm
Bottom circumference (stretched) 44
(51)"/111.5 (129.5)cm
Length (excluding turtleneck) 13 (15)"/33
(38)cm

GAUGE

12 sts and 14 rnds to 4"/10cm over brioche
st using size 10 (6mm) circular needle
(unstretched). **Take time to check gauge.**

BRIOCHE STITCH

(over a multiple of 2 sts)
Rnd 1 *K1, p1; rep from * around.
Rnd 2 *Knit next st in the rnd below, p1;
rep from * around.
Rep rnds 1 and 2 for brioche st.

PONCHO

Beg at bottom edge, with longer circular
needle, cast on 104 (120) sts. Join,
taking care not to twist sts on needle; pm
for beg of rnds. Cont in brioche st and
work even until piece measures 13
(15)"/33 (38)cm from beg. Change to
shorter circular needle.
Neck shaping
Next (dec) rnd *K2tog tbl, p2tog; rep
from * around—52 (60) sts.
Turtleneck
Note Design shown features the WS of
the pat st as the RS of the turtleneck. If
you would like to have the RS of the pat
st as the RS of the turtleneck, turn work
WS out. Cont to work in the rnd as foll:
Beg with rnd 1, cont in brioche st for
11"/28cm. Bind off loosely in k1, p1 rib. ✤

cream of the crop

A wrap-front shrug knit in a luscious angora and wool
blend yarn is the ultimate in luxurious comfort.

bohemian wrapsody

Free and easy is the name of the game
in this playful tasseled poncho.

bohemian wrapsody

WHAT YOU NEED

Yarn
CottonTail **by Jil Eaton/Classic Elite Yarns**, 1¾oz/50g balls, each approx 90yd/82m (cotton)
• 9 (10) balls in #7535 lime

Needles
• **One size 8 (5mm) circular needle, 29"/74cm long,** or size to obtain gauge
• **One size 8 (5mm) circular needle, 16"/40cm long**

Notions
• **Stitch markers**
• **Tapestry needle**

Skill Level
●●●○

HOODED PONCHO

Many knitters insist they can't or won't knit during the summer or make garments for warmer weather. If you fall into that group, give cotton a try! It takes color beautifully and feels cool and comfortable when worn. This lightweight cotton cover-up is perfect for the beach or a summer concert.

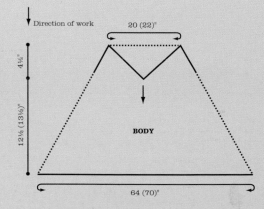

SIZES

Instructions are written for size Small/Medium. Changes for Large/X-Large are in parentheses. (Shown in size Small/Medium.)

FINISHED MEASUREMENTS

Circumference at neck 20 (22)"/51 (56)cm
Circumference at bottom 64 (70)"/162.5 (177.5)cm
Length 17 (18)"/43 (45.5)cm

GAUGE

16 sts and 20 rows (rnds) to 4"/10cm over St st using size 8 (5mm) circular needle. **Take time to check gauge.**

NOTES

1) Poncho is worked in one piece from the top down.
2) To work increases into both lace st pats, work first inc as a single purl st. When a second st has been increased, work both sts into lace st pats as est.

PURSE STITCH

(multiple of 2 sts, worked back and forth)
Row 1 *Yo, p2tog; rep from * across.
Rep row 1 for purse st.

DIAGONAL MESH STITCH

(multiple of 2 sts, worked in the rnd)
Rnd 1 *Yo, p2tog; rep from * around.
Rnd 2 P1, *yo, p2tog; rep from * around, end p1.
Rep rnds 1–2 for diagonal mesh st.

HOOD

Using 16"/40cm circular needle, cast on 80 (88) sts. Work back and forth.
Row 1 (RS) K4, *yo, p2tog; rep from *, end k4.
Row 2 (WS) P4, *yo, p2tog; rep from *, end p4.
Rep rows 1 and 2 until piece measures 14 (15)"/35.5 (38)cm, ending with row 2.
Neckband
Work 4 rows St st.

PONCHO

Yoke
Row 1 (RS) K4, pm, *k 18 (22) sts, pm; rep from * 3 times more, end k4.
Row 2 (WS) Purl, slipping markers.
Row (inc) 3 (RS) K4 left front border sts, sl marker, yo, work purse st to 1 st before marker, yo, k1, sl marker, *k1, yo, work purse st to 1 st before marker, yo, k1, sl marker; rep from * once more, k1, yo, work purse st to last marker, yo, sl marker, k4 right front border sts; inc 8 sts—88 (96) sts.
Row 4 (WS) P4, sl marker, *work purse st to 1 st before marker, p1, sl marker, p1; rep from * 2 times more, work purse st to last marker, sl marker, p4.
Rep rows 3 and 4 nine times more, keeping 1 st each side of marker in St st (k on RS, p on WS)—160 (168) sts.
Next (inc) row (RS) K4, sl marker, *yo, k to 1 st before marker, yo, k1, sl marker, k1; rep from * 2 times more, yo, k to last marker, yo, sl marker, k4—168 (176) sts. Join and pm to beg work in the rnd.
Rnd 1 Knit.
Rnd (inc) 2 K4, sl marker, yo, *k to 1 st before marker, yo, k1, sl marker, k1, yo; rep from * 2 times more, k to last marker, yo, sl marker, k4—176 (184) sts.
Rnds 3–12 Rep rnds 1 and 2 five times more—216 (224) sts.
Rnd 13 K4, sl marker, *work diagonal mesh st to 1 st before marker, k1, sl marker, k1, rep from * 2 times more, work diagonal mesh st to last marker, sl marker, k4.
Rnd 14 (inc) K4, sl marker, yo, *work diagonal mesh st to 1 st before marker, yo, k1, sl marker, k1, yo, rep from * 2 times more, work diagonal mesh st to last marker, yo, sl marker, k4.
Rnds 15–24 Rep rnds 13 and 14 four (six) times more—256 (280) sts.
Rnd 25 Knit.
Rnd 26 K4, sl marker, yo, k2tog, *k to 3 sts before marker, SKP, yo, k1, sl marker, k1, yo, k2tog; rep from * 2 times more, k to 2 sts before marker, SKP, yo, sl marker, k4.
Rep rnds 25 and 26 five times more.
Next rnd K4, sl marker, *p to 1 st before marker, k1, sl marker, k1; rep from * two times more, p to marker, sl marker, k4.
Next rnd K4, sl marker, *yo, p2tog, p to 3 sts before marker, sl 1, p1, psso, yo, k1, sl marker, k1; rep from * 2 times more, yo, p2tog, p to 2 sts before marker, p2tog, yo, sl marker, k4.
Rep last 2 rnds five times more.
Rep rnds 25 and 26 six times more.
Purl 5 rnds. Bind off in purl.

FINISHING

Fold top of hood in half and sew together. Make five 4"/10cm tassels and attach to corners of poncho and to top of hood. ❧

silver lining

Take your look from day to evening in this
subtly shimmering ensemble.

silver lining

WHAT YOU NEED

Yarn
Ultra Alpaca Light **by Berroco, 1¾oz/50g hanks, each approx 144yd/133m (alpaca/wool)**
• 6 (7, 8, 9) hanks in #4209 moonshadow (B)
Metallic FX **by Berroco, .85oz/25g hanks, each approx 85yd/78m (rayon/metallic)**
• **Crop top: 1 hank in #1002 silver (A)**
• **Cowl: 5 hanks in #1002 silver (A)**

Needles
• **Size 7 (4.5mm) circular needles, 16"/40cm long and 24"/60cm long,** or size to obtain gauge
• **Size 6 (4mm) circular needle, 16"/40cm long,** or size to obtain gauge
• **One set (5) each sizes 6 and 7 (4 and 4.5mm) double-pointed needles (dpns)**

Notions
• **Stitch holders**
• **Stitch marker**

Skill Level
●●●●

CROP TOP AND COWL SET

Fine-weight alpaca yarn in a lacy rib pattern provides warmth without bulk for a sleekly flattering silhouette. I accented the neckline with metallic yarn and created a matching silver cowl to add a little glam to the look.

SIZES

Instructions are written for size Small. Changes for Medium, Large, and X-Large are in parentheses. (Shown in size Small.)

FINISHED MEASUREMENTS

Crop top
Bust 35½ (40, 44¼, 48)"/90 (101.5, 112.5, 122)cm
Length (including neckband) 13 (14, 15, 16)"/33 (35.5, 38, 40.5)cm
Upper arm 12¾ (14, 15½, 16¾)"/32.5 (35.5, 39.5, 42.5)cm
Cowl
Circumference 22"/56cm
Width 7½"/19cm

GAUGES

Crop top
22 sts and 28 rnds to 4"/10cm over picot rib using B and size 7 (4.5mm) circular needle (slightly stretched).
Cowl
35 sts and 32 rnds to 4"/10cm over picot rib using A and size 6 (4mm) circular needle (unstretched). **Take time to check gauges.**

NOTES

1) Crop top is worked in one piece from the neckband down.
2) Cowl is worked in the rnd. Cast-on and bound-off edges are stitched together, forming a ring.
3) Schematic is on page 155.

PICOT RIB

(over a multiple of 4 sts)
Rnds 1–5 *K2, p2; rep from * around.
Rnd 6 *Yo, SKP, p2; rep from * around.
Rep rnds 1–6 for picot rib.

CROP TOP

Neckband
With shorter larger circular needle and A, cast on 96 (104, 112, 120) sts. Join, taking care not to twist sts on needle; pm for beg of rnds. Work around in k1, p1 rib for 6 rnds.
Yoke
Change to B.
Next rnd K 38 (42, 46, 50) sts (front), pm, k 10 sts (left sleeve), pm, k 38 (42, 46, 50) sts (back), pm, k 10 sts (right sleeve). Beg with rnd 1, cont in picot rib as foll:
Inc rnd K1, yo, *work picot rib to 1 st before next marker, yo, k1, sl marker, k1, yo; rep from * around 3 times more, end work picot rib to 1 st before rnd marker, yo, k1—104 (112, 120, 128) sts.
Next rnd K1, *work picot rib to 1 st before next marker, k1, slip marker, k1; rep from * around 3 times more, end work picot rib to

1 st before rnd marker, k1. Working new sts into picot rib and changing to longer, larger circular needle when needed, rep last 2 rnds 29 (33, 37, 40) times more—336 (376, 416, 448) sts.
Dividing for body and sleeves
Cont to work in picot rib as established, cont as foll:
Next rnd Work across first 98 (110, 122, 132) sts, place next 70 (78, 86, 92) sts on holder for sleeve, work across next 98 (110, 122, 132) sts, place last 70 (78, 86, 92) sts on holder for sleeve—196 (220, 244, 264) sts. Join and pm for beg of rnds. Cont to work around in picot rib as established until next rnd 6 is completed. Cont in rib (omitting rnd 6 of picot rib), dec sts at each side if necessary to reconcile rib pat and work until piece measures 4"/10cm from dividing rnd. Bind off loosely in rib.
Sleeves
Upper arm
With RS facing, larger dpns, and B, work in picot rib as established over 70 (78, 86, 92) sts from sleeve holder, dividing sts over 4 needles. Join and pm for beg of rnds. Work even for 10"/25.5cm. Mark last rnd.
Forearm
Change to smaller dpns.
Next (dec) rnd K 3 (0, 0, 0), *k1, k2tog; rep from * around, end k1 (0, 2, 2)—48 (52, 58, 62) sts.
Next 5 rnds Knit.
Next (dec) rnd K2tog, knit to last 2 sts, end ssk.
Next 5 rnds Knit. Rep last 6 rnds 0 (0, 1, 2) times more—46 (50, 54, 56) sts. Work even in St st (knit every rnd) until piece measures 10½ (10¼, 11, 11)"/26.5 (26.5, 28, 28)cm above marked rnd.
Cuff
Work in k1, p1 rib for 2"/5cm. For thumb opening, work back and forth in rib pat as established for 1"/2.5cm, end with a WS row. Cont to work around in k1, p1 rib for 2"/5cm. Bind off loosely in rib.

COWL

With smaller, shorter circular needle and A, cast on 132 sts. Join, taking care not to twist sts on needle; pm for beg of rnds. Work around in picot rib for 22"/56cm, end with rnd 6. Bind off in pat st. Sew bound-off edge to cast-on edge forming a ring. ❖

criss crop

This simple-shaped top is all about the dense cable pattern
that criss-crosses the entire fabric.

criss crop

WHAT YOU NEED

Yarn
Puffin **by Quince & Co.**, 3½oz/100g hanks, each approx 112yd/102m (wool)
• 7 (8, 9, 11) hanks each in #108 delft

Needles
• **Size 13 (9mm) circular needles, one 16"/40cm long and three 29"/74cm long,** or size to obtain gauge

Notions
• **Cable needle (cn)**
• **Stitch marker**

Skill Level
●●●○

LATTICE CABLE CROP TOP
Rather than combining several stitch patterns, as I often like to do, I let the lattice cable stitch take center stage here. It's a bold stitch, especially when worked in a chunky yarn.

SIZES
Instructions are written for size Small. Changes for Medium, Large, and X-Large are in parentheses. (Shown in size Small.)

FINISHED MEASUREMENTS
Bust 38¼ (43¼, 49¼, 55¼)"/97 (110, 125, 140.5)cm
Length 16½ (17, 17, 18)"/42 (43, 43, 45.5)cm
Upper arm 17 (18, 18, 20)"/43 (45.5, 45.5, 51)cm

GAUGE
17 sts and 14 rnds to 4"/10cm over lattice cable using size 13 (9mm) circular needle.
Take time to check gauge.

NOTES
1) Body is worked in the rnd to armholes, then back and front bodices are worked back and forth.
2) Front bodice is 6 sts wider than back bodice.
3) Sleeves are worked in the round.

STITCH GLOSSARY
4-st RC Sl 2 sts to cn and hold to **back**, k2, k2 from cn.

4-st LC Sl 2 sts to cn and hold to **front**, k2, k2 from cn.

4-st RPC Sl 2 sts to cn and hold to **back**, k2, p2 from cn.

4-st LPC Sl 2 sts to cn and hold to **front**, p2, k2 from cn.

LATTICE CABLE
(over a multiple of 6 sts)
Rnd (row) 1 *K4, p2; rep from * to end.
Rnd (row) 2 and all even rnds (rows) K the knit sts and p the purl sts.
Rnd (row) 3 *4-st RC, p2; rep from * to end.
Rnd (row) 5 P2, *k2, 4-st RPC; rep from * to last 4 sts, end k4.
Rnd (row) 7 *P2, 4-st LC; rep from * to end.
Rnd (row) 9 K4, *4-st LPC, k2; rep from * to last 2 sts, end p2.
Rnd (row) 10 Rep rnd 2.
Rep rnds (rows) 1–10 for lattice cable.

BODY
With longer circular needle, cast on 162 (186, 210, 234) sts. Join and pm for beg of rnds. Cont in lattice cable until piece measures 8"/20.5cm from beg, end with an even numbered rnd.

Back bodice
With 2nd longer circular needle, work next row of lattice cable over first 78 (90, 102, 114) sts; leave rem 84 (96, 108, 120) sts on first needle for front bodice (make note of which rnd you ended on). Cont to work back and forth in lattice cable using 2 circular needles until armhole measures 8½ (9, 9, 10)"/21.5 (23, 23, 25.5)cm, end with a WS row. Bind off in pat st.

Front bodice
Using 2 longer circular needles, work back and forth on 84 (96, 108, 120) sts until armhole measures 7½ (8, 8½, 9)"/19 (20.5, 21.5, 23)cm, end with a WS row (make note of what row you ended on to work neckband).

Neck shaping
Next row (RS) Work across first 24 (30, 36, 42) sts, place center 36 sts on a shorter circular needle, join a 2nd ball of yarn and work across last 24 (30, 36, 42) sts. Working both sides at once, work even until piece measures same length as back to shoulder, end with a WS row. Bind off each side in pat st.

SLEEVES
With rem shorter circular needle, cast on 72 (78, 78, 84) sts. Join, taking care not to twist sts on needle; pm for beg of rnds. Work around in lattice cable until piece measures 8 (9, 9, 10)"/20.5 (23, 23, 25.5)cm from beg, end with an odd-numbered rnd. Bind off in pat st.

FINISHING
Sew shoulder seams.

Neckband
With RS facing and using LH end of circular needle holding front neck sts, join yarn and pick up and k 3 sts along right neck edge, 30 sts along back neck edge, then 3 sts along left neck edge—72 sts. Join and pm for beg of rnds. Beg with next odd-numbered rnd, work around in lattice cable pat for 5 rnds. Bind off in pat st. Set sleeves into armholes. ✤

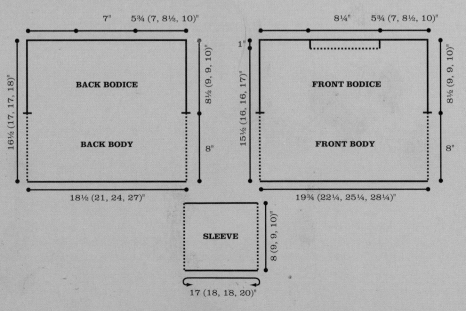

bold & beautiful

Super-chunky yarn and a graphic color
pattern create a showstopping look.

bold & beautiful

WHAT YOU NEED

Yarn

Magnum **by Cascade Yarns, 8¾oz/250g hanks, each approx 123yd/112m (Peruvian highland wool)** ⑥
- **3 (4) hanks in #9431 regal red (A)**
- **2 (3) hanks in #9421 blue hawaii (B)**

Needles
- **Two each size 15 (10mm) circular needles, 16"/40cm and 29"/74cm long,** or size to obtain gauge

Notions
- **Stitch markers**

Skill Level

●●●○

BULKY FAIR ISLE SHRUG

This boldly patterned shrug works up quickly. The sleeves are knit from side to side and then joined in the center front, after which stitches are picked up around the neck opening for the collar.
Although the colors are inspired by Native American textiles, the stitch pattern is actually blown-up Fair Isle.

SIZES

Instructions are written for size Small/Medium. Changes for Large/X-Large are in parentheses. (Shown in size Small/Medium.)

FINISHED MEASUREMENTS

Bust 36 (44)"/91.5 (111.5)cm
Length 11½ (12½)"/29 (31.5)cm
Upper arm 20 (22)"/51 (56)cm

GAUGE

11 sts and 13 rnds to 5"/12.5cm over chart pats using size 15 (10mm) circular needle.
Take time to check gauge.

NOTES

1) Each sleeve is worked in the rnd to underarm, then the body section is worked back and forth.
2) To work in the rnd, always read chart from right to left.
3) Charts are on page 156.

SEED STITCH

(over a multiple of 2 sts)
Rnd 1 *K1, p1; rep from * around.
Rnd 2 K the purl sts and p the knit sts.
Rep rnd 2 for seed st.

LEFT HALF

Sleeve
Beg at bottom edge, holding two shorter circular needles tog (to allow for a loose cast-on), cast on 44 (48) sts using the backward-loop method and alternating A and B. Remove one needle, then join and pm for beg of rnds. Cont in rib as foll:
Rnds 1 and 2 *P1 with A, k1 with B; rep from * around.
Beg chart pat 1 (see page 156 for charts)
Rnd 1 Work 4-st rep 11 (12) times. Cont to foll chart in this way to rnd 8.
Beg chart pat 2
Rnd 1 Work 4-st rep 11 (12) times. Cont to foll chart in this way to rnd 9.
Beg chart pat 3
Rnd 1 Work 4-st rep 11 (12) times. Cont to foll chart in this way to rnd 10.
Beg chart pat 4
Rnd 1 Work 4-st rep 11 (12) times. Cont to foll chart in this way to rnd 4.
For size Small/Medium only
Rep rnds 1–3 once more.
For size Large/X-Large only
Rep rnds 1–4, then rnds 1 and 2 once.
Body
For all sizes
Using two longer circular needles, work back and forth in stripe pat as foll:
Row 1 (RS) With A, knit.
Row 2 With A, purl. **Row 3** With B, knit.
Row 4 With B, purl. Rep these 4 rows 5 (6) times more. Bind off with B.

RIGHT HALF

Sleeve
Cast on and work ribbing as for left sleeve. Change to B and work in St st for 2 rnds.
Beg chart pat 5
Rnd 1 Work 4-st rep 11 (12) times. Cont to foll chart in this way to rnd 10.
Beg chart pat 6
Rnd 1 Work 4-st rep 11 (12) times. Cont to foll chart in this way to rnd 9.
Beg chart pat 1
Rnd 1 Work 4-st rep 11 (12) times. Cont to foll chart in this way to rnd 8.
Beg chart pat 4
Rnd 1 Work 4-st rep 11 (12) times. Cont to foll chart in this way to rnd 4.
For size Small/Medium only
Rep rnd 1 once more.
For size Large/X-Large only
Rep rnds 1–4 once more.
Body (all sizes)
Using two longer circular needles, work back and forth in stripe pat as foll:
Row 1 (RS) With B, knit.
Row 2 With B, purl. **Row 3** With A, knit.
Row 4 With A, purl. Rep these 4 rows 5 (6) times more. Bind off with A.

FINISHING

Working from the bottom edge up, use B to whipstitch the halves together with a 3 (4)"/7.5 (10)cm long seam on back and front.
Collar
With RS facing, longer circular needle, and A, beg at center back seam and pick up and k 33 sts evenly spaced along left neck edge to center front seam, then pick up and k 33 sts evenly spaced along right neck edge to center back seam—66 sts. Join and pm for beg of rnds. Work around in seed st for 10 (11)"/25.5 (28)cm. Bind off loosely in seed st.
Bottom band
With RS facing, longer circular needle, and A, beg at center of right underarm and pick up and k 52 (63) sts evenly spaced along front bottom edge to center of left underarm, then pick up and k 52 (63) sts evenly spaced along back bottom edge to center of right underarm—104 (126) sts. Join and pm for beg of rnds. Work around in seed st for 3 rnds. Bind off loosely in seed st. ✤

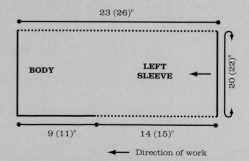

23 (26)"

BODY | LEFT SLEEVE

20 (22)"

9 (11)" | 14 (15)"

← Direction of work

snow wonder

Sleigh rides and sipping hot chocolate by the fire call out for a wintry number like this.

snow wonder

WHAT YOU NEED

Yarn
Ribbon Ball **by Be Sweet, 1¾oz/50g skeins, each approx 95yd/87m (hand-dyed baby mohair/metallic with hand-tied ribbon)**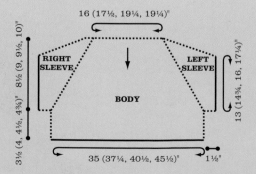
- **3 (3, 3, 4) skeins in #49 natural (A)**

Handspun Merino **by Be Sweet, 3½oz/100g skeins, each approx 65yd/59m (merino wool)**
- **4 (4, 5, 5) skeins in #49 natural (B)**

Needles
- **One size 10½ (6.5mm) circular needle, 24"/60cm long,** or size to obtain gauge
- **Two size 10½ (6.5mm) circular needles, 16"/40cm long**

Notions
- **Stitch markers**
- **Tapestry needle**

Skill Level
●●●●

BOBBLED PULLOVER
What better way to combat a gray winter day than to don a bobbled and beribboned topper? It's easier to knit than it might look, as the increases in the textured yoke are simply integrated into the bells and bobbles.

SIZES
Instructions are written for size Small. Changes for Medium, Large, and X-Large are in parentheses. (Shown in size Small.)

FINISHED MEASUREMENTS
Bust at underarm 35 (37¼, 40½, 45½)"/89 (94.5, 103, 115.5)cm
Back length 12 (13, 14, 14¾)"/30.5 (33, 35.5, 37.5)cm

GAUGES
10 sts and 12 rnds to 4"/10cm over St st using A (double stranded) and size 10½ (6.5mm) circular needle.
13 sts and 20 rnds to 4"/10cm over rev St st using B and size 10½ (6.5mm) circular needle.
15 sts and 20 rows = 4"/10cm over Canterbury bells pat using B and size 10½ (6.5mm) circular needle. **Take time to check gauges.**

NOTES
1) Garment is worked from the top down in the rnd.
2) Stitch count varies with the Canterbury bells pattern st. All instruction counts are based on the original multiple.

STITCH GLOSSARY
K1b Inc 1 st by knitting in the row below the st and then knitting the st itself.
M7 Knit into front and back of st 3 times, then into front again.
MB (Make Bobble) Knit into the front and back of st until there are 6 loops on RH needle. Pass the first 5 loops over the last loop. Return st to LH needle and knit it.

K1, P1 RIB
(over a multiple of 2 sts)
Rnd 1 *K1, p1; rep from * around.
Rep rnd 1 for k1, p1 rib.

CANTERBURY BELLS
(over a multiple of 6 sts)

Rnd 1 *P2, k1, p2, m7; rep from * around.
Rnd 2 *P2, k1, p2, k7-tbl; rep from * around.
Rnd 3 *P2, k1, p2, k5, k2tog; rep from * around.
Rnd 4 *P2, k1, p2, k4, k2tog; rep from * around.
Rnd 5 *P2, k1, p2, k3, k2tog; rep from * around.
Rnd 6 *P2, k1, p2, k2, k2tog; rep from * around.
Rnd 7 *P2, k1, p2, k1, k2tog; rep from * around.
Rnd 8 *P2, k1, p2, k2tog; rep from * around.
Rnd 9 *P2, k1, p3; rep from * around.
Rep rnds 1–9 for Canterbury bells pat.

PULLOVER
Collar
With longer circular needle and 2 strands of A held together, cast on 96 (102, 108, 108) sts. Pm and join, being careful not to twist sts.
Rnd 1 K 48 (51, 54, 54) sts, pm (halfway), k to end.
Rnd 2 K2tog, k to 2 sts before halfway marker, SKP, k2tog, k to 2 sts before end marker, SKP—92 (98, 104, 104) sts.
Rep rnds 1 and 2 8 times more—60 (66, 72, 72) sts.
Work in St st (k every rnd) for 2½"/6.5cm more.
Change to k1, p1 rib and work for 3½"/9cm.
Yoke
Change to B.
Rnds 1 and 2 Knit.
Rnd 3 *P2, k1, p2, m7; rep from * around.
Rnd 4 *P2, k1, p2, k7-tbl; rep from * around.
Rnd 5 (inc #1) *P2, k1b, p2, k5, k2tog; rep from * around—70 (77, 84, 84) sts.
Rnd 6 *P2, k2, p2, k4, k2tog; rep from * around.
Rnd 7 *P2, k2, p2, k3, k2tog; rep from * around.
Rnd 8 (inc #2) *P2, k1, yo, k1, p2, k2, k2tog; rep from * around—80 (88, 96, 96) sts.
Rnd 9 *P2, k1, MB, k1, p2, k1, k2tog; rep from * around.
Rnd 10 *P2, k1, k1-tbl, k1, p2, k2tog; rep from * around.

Direction of work

RIGHT SLEEVE

LEFT SLEEVE

BODY

16 (17½, 19¼, 19¼)"

8½ (9, 9½, 10)"

3½ (4, 4½, 4¾)"

13 (14¾, 16, 17¼)"

35 (37¼, 40½, 45½)"

1½"

Rnd 11 (inc #3 & 4) *p2, k1, yo, k1, yo, k1, p3; rep from * around—100 (110, 120, 120) sts.

Rnd 12 *P2, k1, p1, k1, p1, k1, p2, m7; rep from * around.

Rnd 13 *P2, k1, MB, k1, MB, k1, p2, k7-tbl; rep from * around.

Rnd 14 *P2, k1, p1, k1, p1, k1, p2, k5, k2tog; rep from * around.

Rnd 15 *P2, k1, p1, k1, p1, k1, p2, k4, k2tog; rep from * around.

Rnd 16 (inc #5) *P2, k1, p1, k1b, p1, k1, p2, k3, k2tog; rep from * around—110 (121, 132, 132) sts.

Rnd 17 *P2, k1, MB, k2, MB, k1, p2, k2, k2tog; rep from * around.

Rnd 18 *P2, k1, p1, k2, p1, k1, p2, k1, k2tog; rep from * around.

Rnd 19 (inc #6 & 7) *P2, k1, p1, (k1b) 2 times, p1, k1, p2, k2tog; rep from * around—130 (143, 156, 156) sts.

Rnd 20 (inc #8) *P2, k1, p1, k2, yo, k2, p1, k1, p3; rep from * around—140 (154, 168, 168) sts.

Rnd 21 *P2, k1, MB, k2, MB, k2, MB, k1, p2, m7; rep from * around.

Rnd 22 *P2, k1, p1, k2, p1, k2, p1, k1, p2, k7-tbl; rep from * around.

Rnd 23 *P2, k1, p1, k2, p1, k2, p1, k1, p2, k5, k2tog; rep from * around.

Rnd 24 *P2, k1, p1, k2, p1, k2, p1, k1, p2, k4, k2tog; rep from * around.

Rnd 25 *P2, yo, SKP, MB, k1, p1, k1, MB, k2tog, yo, p2, k3, k2tog; rep from * around.

Rnd 26 *P3, (k1, p1) 3 times, k1, p3, k2, k2tog; rep from * around.

Rnd 27 *P3, yo, SKP, k1, p1, k1, k2tog, yo, p3, k1, k2tog; rep from * around.

Rnd 28 (inc #9 & 10) *Yo, p4, k2, MB, k2, p4, yo, k2tog; rep from * around—160 (176, 192, 192) sts.

Rnd 29 *P5, yo, SKP, k1-tbl, k2tog, yo, p6; rep from * around.

Rnd 30 *P6, k3, p6, m7; rep from * around.

Rnd 31 *P6, m1, k3tog-tbl, m1, p6, k7-tbl; rep from * around.

Rnd 32 *P15, k5, k2tog; rep from * around.

Rnd 33 *P15, k4, k2tog; rep from * around.

Rnd 34 (inc #11 & 12) *Yo, p15, yo, k3, k2tog; rep from * around—180 (198, 216, 216) sts.

Rnd 35 *P17, k2, k2tog; rep from * around.

Rnd 36 *P17, k1, k2tog; rep from * around.

Rnd 37 *P17, k2tog; rep from * around.

Rnd 38 *P17, k1b; rep from * around—190 (209, 228, 228) sts.

For sizes S, M, & L only
Cont to purl around, until drop from shoulder measures 8½ (9, 9½, 10)"/21.5 (22¾, 24, 25) cm or desired length. Cont to yoke divide.

For size X-Large only
Rnd 39 Purl.

Rnd 40 *P17, (k1b) 2 times; rep from * around—252 sts.
Cont to purl around, until drop from shoulder measures 10"/25.5cm or desired length. Cont to yoke divide.

Divide yoke
The tapered ends of the boat neck have to be centered over the sleeves, so the order of the yoke-divide is important: Slip the first 20 (23, 25, 27) sts (half of the first sleeve) onto a 16"/40cm circular needle and hold aside. Break yarn and reattach yarn to separate the remainder of the yoke as follows: Using the main circular needle, p 55 (59, 64, 72) front sts, cast on 2 sts at underarm, slip the next 40 (46, 50, 54) sleeve sts onto a shorter circular needle and hold aside. P 55 (58, 64, 72) back sts, cast on 2 sts at underarm, slip the final 20 (23, 25, 27) sts for the second half of the first sleeve onto the first sleeve circular needle.

Body
With WS facing, pm at beg of rnd—114 (121, 132, 148) sts and knit 16 (18, 20, 22) rnds.

Next rnd *K1, yo; rep from * around. Work 2 rnds of k1, p1 rib. Bind off in rib.

Sleeves
With WS facing and working in the round, cast on 2 sts at underarm and pm between the 2—42 (48, 52, 56) sts. Knit 6 rnds. Work 2 rnds of k1, p1 Rib. Bind off in rib.
Rep for second sleeve.

FINISHING
Sew body and sleeves together at underarm. ❧

eyelet candy

Slip into warmth with this sumptuous topper. Knit in candy-apple red, it will get your heart racing.

eyelet candy

WHAT YOU NEED

Yarn
Brushed Suri **by Blue Sky Alpacas,
1¾oz/50g hanks, each approx 142yd/130m
(baby suri alpaca/merino wool/bamboo)**
• 5 (6, 6) hanks in #902 lollipop (MC)
Worsted Hand Dyes **by Blue Sky Alpacas,
3½oz/100g hanks, each approx 100yd/91m
(royal alpaca/merino wool)** 4
• 2 hanks in #2026 petunia (CC)

Needles
• **Size 9 (5.5mm) circular needles,
16"/40cm long and 24"/61cm long**, or size
to obtain gauge
• **One set (5) size 9 (5.5mm) double-pointed
needles (dpns)**

Notions
• **Stitch marker**

Skill Level
●●○○

RUCHED WRAP
Two alpaca-wool blend yarns (one with a
bit of bamboo) combine to create a super-
soft warmer. I wasn't going for a retro vibe
when I designed this wrap, but I like the
old-fashioned glamour that a stole evokes.

SIZES
Instructions are written for size Small.
Changes for Medium and Large are in
parentheses. (Shown in size Small.)

FINISHED MEASUREMENTS
Circumference 39 (43, 47)"/99 (109,
119.5)cm
Width of narrowest eyelet band 7"/18cm
Width of widest eyelet band 16"/40.5cm

GAUGE
14 sts and 16 rnds to 4"/10cm over St st
using MC and size 9 (5.5mm) circular
needle. **Take time to check gauge.**

NOTE
Wrap is made in one piece, beginning
and ending at eyelet band 1 (narrowest
eyelet band).

STITCH GLOSSARY
kf&b Inc 1 by knitting into the front and
back of the next st.

WRAP
Eyelet band 1
With dpn and CC, cast on 48 sts. Divide
sts over 4 needles. Join, taking care not to
twist sts on needles; pm for beg of rnds.
Rnd 1 Knit.
Rnd 2 Purl.
Rnd 3 *K1, p1; rep from * around.
Rnd 4 K1, *yo, SKP; rep from * around,
end p1.
Rnd 5 *K1, p1; rep from * around.
Rnd 6 Purl.
Next (inc) rnd *K3, kf&b; rep from *
around—60 sts. Change to MC.
Next rnd Knit. Change to shorter
circular needle.
Next (inc) rnd *K1, M1; rep from *
around—120 sts.
Next 6 rnds Knit.
Next (dec) rnd *K2tog tbl; rep from *
around—60 sts.
Eyelet band 2
With CC, work rnds 1–6 of eyelet band 1.

Next (inc) rnd *K4, kf&b; rep from *
around—72 sts. Change to MC.
Next rnd Knit. Change to longer circular
needle.
Next (inc) rnd *K1, M1; rep from *
around—144 sts.
Next 8 rnds Knit. Change to shorter
circular needle.
Next (dec) rnd *K2tog tbl; rep from *
around—72 sts.
Eyelet band 3
With CC, work rnds 1–6 of eyelet band 1.
Next (inc) rnd *K5, kf&b; rep from *
around—84 sts. Change to MC.
Next rnd Knit. Change to longer circular
needle.
Next (inc) rnd *K1, M1; rep from *
around—168 sts.
Next 10 rnds Knit.
Next (dec) rnd *K2tog tbl; rep from *
around—84 sts.
Eyelet band 4
With CC, work rnds 1–6 of eyelet band 1.
Next (inc) rnd *K6, kf&b; rep from *
around—96 sts. Change to MC.
Next rnd Knit.
Next (inc) rnd *K1, M1; rep from *
around—192 sts.
Next 12 rnds Knit.
Next (dec) rnd *K2tog tbl; rep from *
around—96 sts.
Eyelet band 5
With CC, work as foll:
Rnd 1 Knit.
Rnd 2 Purl.
Rnd 3 *K1, p1; rep from * around.
Rnd 4 K1, *yo, SKP; rep from * around,
end p1.
Rnd 5 *K1, p1; rep from * around.
Rnd 6 Purl. **Rnd 7** Knit. Change to MC.
Next rnd Knit.
Next (inc) rnd *K1, M1; rep from *
around—192 sts.
Next 12 rnds Knit.
Next (dec) rnd *K2tog tbl; rep from *
around—96 sts. Rep eyelet band 5 two (3,
4) times more.
Eyelet band 6
With CC, work as foll:
Rnd (dec) 1 *K6, k2tog; rep from *
around—84 sts.
Rnd 2 Purl.
Rnd 3 *K1, p1; rep from * around.
Rnd 4 K1, *yo, SKP; rep from * around,
end p1.

Rnd 5 *K1, p1; rep from * around.

Rnd 6 Purl.

Rnd 7 Knit. Change to MC.

Next rnd Knit.

Next (inc) rnd *K1, M1; rep from * around—168 sts.

Next 10 rnds Knit.

Next (dec) rnd *K2tog tbl; rep from * around—84 sts. Change to shorter circular needle.

Eyelet band 7

With CC, work as foll:

Rnd (dec) 1 *K5, k2tog; rep from * around—72 sts. Rep rnds 2–7 as for eyelet band 6. Change to MC.

Next rnd Knit. Change to longer circular needle.

Next (inc) rnd *K1, M1; rep from * around—144 sts.

Next 8 rnds Knit. Change to shorter circular needle.

Next (dec) rnd *K2tog tbl; rep from * around—72 sts.

Eyelet band 8

With CC, work as foll:

Rnd (dec) 1 *K4, k2tog; rep from * around—60 sts. Rep rnds 2–7 as for eyelet band 6. Change to MC.

Next rnd Knit. Change to longer circular needle.

Next (inc) rnd *K1, M1; rep from * around—120 sts.

Next 6 rnds Knit. Change to shorter circular needle.

Next (dec) rnd *K2tog tbl; rep from * around—60 sts.

Eyelet band 9

Change to dpns. With CC, work as foll:

Rnd (dec) 1 *K3, k2tog; rep from * around—48 sts. Rep rnds 2–7 as for eyelet band 6. Change to MC.

Next rnd Knit. Change to longer circular needle.

Next (inc) rnd *K1, M1; rep from * around—96 sts.

Next 4 rnds Knit. Change to dpns.

Next (dec) rnd *K2tog tbl; rep from * around—48 sts. Bind off knitwise; cut yarn, leaving a long tail for sewing.

FINISHING

Using MC tail, sew bound-off edge to cast-on edge of eyelet band 1. ❖

crème de la crème

Luscious yarn and a stunning stitch pattern create a decadent cover-up.
The optional arm warmers are the pièce de résistance.

crème de la crème

Yarn
Bulky **by Blue Sky Alpacas, 3½oz/100g
hanks, each approx 45yd/41m (alpaca/
wool) in #1002 silver mink**
- **6 (7) hanks for poncho**
- **2 (3) hanks for arm warmers**

Needles
- **Size 15 (10mm) circular needles,
16"/40cm and 29"/74cm long,** or size to
obtain gauge **for poncho**
- **One set (4) size 15 (10mm) double-
pointed needles (dpns)** or size to obtain
gauge **for arm warmers**

Notions
- **Stitch marker**

Skill Level
●●●○

DROP-STITCH PONCHO AND ARM WARMERS

This matching set provides as much cozy
coverage as a sweater, but with tons of
versatility. Knit in a bulky yarn, it works
up quickly, making it an ideal gift.

SIZES

Instructions are written for size
Small/Medium. Changes for Large/
X-Large are in parentheses. (Shown in
size Small/Medium.)

FINISHED MEASUREMENTS

Poncho
Bottom circumference (unstretched)
32 (36)"/81 (91.5)cm
Bottom circumference (stretched)
40 (45)"/101.5 (114.5)cm
Length (excluding turtleneck)
16 (17)"/40.5 (43)cm

Arm warmers
Circumference 8 (9)"/20.5 (23)cm
Length 16"/40.5cm

GAUGES

Poncho
8 sts and 11 rnds to 4"/10cm over drop st
using size 15 (10mm) circular needle.

Arm warmers
9 sts and 11 rnds to 4"/10cm over k1,
p1 rib using size 15 (10mm) dpns
(unstretched). **Take time to check gauges.**

DROP STITCH

(over a multiple of 8 sts)
Rnd 1 *K2, p2; rep from * around.
Rnd 2 *K1, yo, k1, p2, k2, p2; rep from *
around.
Rnds 3–8 K the knit sts and yo's, and p
the purl sts.
Rnd 9 *K1, drop next st and allow it to
unravel, k1, p2, k1, yo, k1, p2; rep from
* around.
Rnds 10–15 Rep rnd 3.
Rnd 16 *K1, yo, k1, p2, k1, drop next st
and allow it to unravel, k1, p2; rep from
* around.
Rnds 1–16 form drop st.

PONCHO

Beg at bottom edge, with longer circular
needle, cast on 64 (72) sts. Join, taking
care not to twist sts on needle, pm for
beg of rnds. Work around in k2, p2 rib
for 1 (4) rnds. Cont in drop st as foll:
work rnds 1–16 once, rnds 3–16 once,
then rnds 3–8 once.
Next rnd *K1, drop next st and allow it
to unravel, k1, p2, k2, p2; rep from *
around.
Neck shaping
Rnd (dec) 1 *K2tog, p2, k2, p2; rep from
* around—56 (63) sts. Change to shorter
circular needle.
Rnds 2 and 3 K the knit sts and p the
purl sts.
Rnd (dec) 4 *K1, p2, k2tog, p2; rep from
* around—48 (54) sts.
Turtleneck
Next rnd K the knit sts and p the purl
sts. Rep this rnd for 11"/28cm. Bind off
in established rib pat.

ARM WARMERS

With dpn, cast on 18 (20) sts. Divide sts
over 3 needles. Join, taking care not to
twist sts on needles; pm for beg of rnds.
Work around in k1, p1 rib for
16"/40.5cm. Bind off loosely in rib. ❖

blue by you

Knit yourself a top pretty enough for a Southern belle
with beautiful blue stripes in a host of lace patterns.

blue by you

WHAT YOU NEED

Yarn
Provence **by Classic Elite Yarns**, 3½oz/100g
hanks, each approx 205yd/186m
(mercerized cotton)
- **2 (3, 3, 3) hanks in #2647 delft blue (A)**
- **2 (3, 3, 3) hanks in #2610 marine (B)**

Needles
- **Three size 5 (3.75mm) circular needles,
24"/60cm long,** or size to obtain gauge
- **Size 5 (3.75mm) circular needle,
16"/40cm long**
- **One set (5) size 5 (3.75mm) double-
pointed needles (dpns)**

Notions
- **Stitch markers**

Skill Level
●●●○

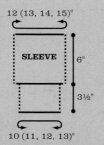

STRIPED LACE PULLOVER
This cropped top is a study in contrasts
pulled together by harmonious two-tone
coloring: clean stripes versus a variety of
frilly laces and an orderly horizontal
design versus the seemingly "unfinished"
hanging lace hem.

SIZES
Instructions are written for size Small.
Changes for Medium, Large, and X-Large
are in parentheses. (Shown in size Small.)

FINISHED MEASUREMENTS
Bust 43 (48, 52, 55½)"/109 (122, 132,
141)cm
Length 12½ (13, 13½, 14)"/32 (33, 34,
35.5)cm
Upper arm 12 (13, 14, 15)"/30.5 (33, 35.5,
38)cm

GAUGE
22 sts and 29 rnds to 4"/10cm over St st
using size 5 (3.75mm) circular needle.
Take time to check gauge.

NOTES
1) Body is worked in the rnd to armholes.
2) Back and front bodices are worked
back and forth.
3) Sleeves are worked in the rnd.

CHEVRON LAYETTE STITCH
(over a multiple of 7 sts plus 1)
Rnd 1 K1, *k2, SK2P, k2, yo; rep from *
around
Rnd 2 K1, *yo, k6; rep from * around.
Rep rnds 1 and 2 for chevron layette st.

IMITATION EMBROIDERY STITCH
(over a multiple of 6 sts plus 2)
Row 1 (RS) P2, *yo, SKP, k2tog, yo, p2;
rep from * to end.
Row 2 K2, *p4, k2; rep from * to end.
Row 3 P2, *k4, p2; rep from * to end.
Row 4 Rep row 2.
Rep rows 1-4 for imitation embroidery st.

MINIATURE LEAF PATTERN
(over a multiple of 6 sts)
Rnd 1 *K3, yo, k3tog, yo; rep from * around.
Rnd 2 Knit.

Rnd 3 *Yo, k3tog, yo, k3; rep from * around.
Rnd 4 Knit.
Rep rnds 1-4 for miniature leaf pat.

CELLULAR STITCH
(over a multiple of 3 sts)
Rnd 1 Knit.
Rnd 2 *K2tog, yo, k1; rep from * around.
Rnd 3 Knit.
Rnd 4 *Yo, k1, k2tog; rep from * around.
Rep rnds 1-4 for cellular st.

BODY
With longer circular needle and A, cast
on 239 (267, 288, 309) sts. Join and pm
for beg of rnds.
Next rnd Knit. Cont in chevron layette st
and work even for 3½"/9cm. Change to B
and cont in St st (knit every rnd) until
piece measures 6½"/16.5cm from beg.
Dividing for back and front bodices
Change to 2nd longer circular needle.
Next row (RS) With B, knit across first
119 (133, 144, 154) sts; leave rem 120
(134, 144, 155) sts on first needle for
front bodice.
Back bodice
Change to A. Working back and forth
using 2 circular needles, cont as foll:
Next row (WS) Purl across, inc 3 (inc 1,
inc 2, dec 2) sts evenly spaced—122
(134, 146, 152) sts. Cont in imitation
embroidery st for 3"/7.5cm, end with a
WS row. Change to B.
Next row (RS) Knit across, dec 2 (0, dec
2, inc 2) sts evenly spaced—120 (134, 144,
154) sts. Beg with a purl row, cont in St st
(knit on RS, purl on WS) until armhole
measures 6 (6½, 7, 7½)"/15 (16.5, 18, 19)cm,
end with a WS row. Bind off all sts.
Front bodice
Change to 2nd longer circular needle.
Next row (RS) With B, knit across 120
(134, 144, 155) sts on first needle. Change
to A. Working back and forth using 2
circular needles, cont as foll:
Next row (WS) Purl across, inc 2 (0,
inc 2, dec 3) sts evenly spaced—122
(134, 146, 152) sts. Cont in imitation
embroidery st for 3"/7.5cm, end with a
WS row. Change to B.
Next row (RS) Knit across, dec 2 (0, dec 2,

inc 2) sts evenly spaced—120 (134, 144, 154) sts. Beg with a purl row, cont in St st until armhole measures 4 (4½, 5, 5½)"/10 (11.5, 12.5, 14)cm, end with a WS row.

Neck shaping

Next row (RS) K 40 (46, 50, 54) sts, join a 2nd ball of B and bind off center 40 (42, 44, 46) sts, knit to end. Working both sides at once, purl next row.

Dec row (RS) With first ball of yarn, knit to last 5 sts, [k2tog] twice, k1; with 2nd ball of yarn, k1, [ssk] twice, knit to end. Purl next row. Rep last 2 rows 4 times more—30 (36, 40, 44) sts each side. Work even until piece measures same length as back to shoulder, end with a WS row. Bind off each side.

RIGHT SLEEVE

With dpn and B, cast on 66 (72, 78, 84) sts. Divide sts over 4 needles. Join, taking care not to twist sts on needles; pm for beg of rnds. Work around in k1, p1 rib for 3½"/9cm. Change to A. Cont in miniature leaf pat and work even for 3"/7.5cm. Change to B. Cont in St st and work even until piece measures 9½"/24cm from beg. Bind off.

LEFT SLEEVE

With dpn and B, cast on 66 (72, 78, 84) sts. Divide sts over 4 needles. Join, taking care not to twist sts on needles; pm for beg of rnds. Work around in k1, p1 rib for 3½"/9cm. Change to A. Cont in cellular st and work even for 3"/7.5cm. Change to B. Cont in St st and work even until piece measures 9½"/24cm from beg. Bind off.

FINISHING

Sew shoulder seams.

Neckband

With RS facing, shorter circular needle, and B, beg at left shoulder seam and pick up and k 11 sts evenly spaced along left front neck edge, 40 (42, 44, 46) sts across front neck edge, 11 sts along right neck edge, then 60 (62, 64, 66) sts across back neck edge—122 (126, 130, 134) sts. Join and pm for beg of rnds. Work around in k1, p1 rib for 6 rnds. Bind off loosely in rib. Set sleeves into armholes. ❧

luxe life

Tiny sequins and beads adorn this lacy silk mohair capelet for a quietly dazzling lo[ok]

luxe life

LACY CAPELET

Tilli Tomas produces some of the classiest and loveliest novelty yarns on the market today. My rule of thumb when designing with embellished fibers is the simpler the shape the better to let the yarn shine.

SIZES

Instructions are written for size Small/Medium. Changes for Large/X-Large are in parentheses. (Shown in size Small/Medium.)

FINISHED MEASUREMENTS

Circumference above ruffle 37 (44)"/94 (112)cm
Length (including ruffle) 14 (15½)"/35.5 (39.5)cm

GAUGE

13 sts and 24 rnds to 4"/10cm over leaf st using 2 strands of yarn A and B held tog and size 8 (5mm) circular needle. **Take time to check gauge.**

NOTES

1) Capelet is worked from the neck down.
2) Neckband and body are worked using 2 strands of yarn held tog.
3) Ruffle is worked using one strand of yarn.

STITCH GLOSSARY

kf&b Inc 1 by knitting into the front and back of the next st.

LEAF STITCH

(over a multiple of 6 sts)
Rnd 1 *K3, yo, k3tog, yo; rep from* around.
Rnd 2 Knit.
Rnd 3 *Yo, k3tog, yo, k3; rep from* around.
Rnd 4 Knit.
Rep rnds 1–4 for leaf st.

CAPELET

Neckband
With shorter circular needle, and A and B held tog, cast on 60 (72) sts. Join and pm for beg of rnds.
Rnd 1 Purl.
Rnds 2 and 4 Knit.
Rnds 3 and 5 Purl.
Rnd (inc) 6 *K2, yo; rep from * around—90 (108) sts.
Rnd 7 Purl. Change to longer circular needle.
Rnd (inc) 8 *K3, yo; rep from * around—120 (144) sts.
Rnd 9 Purl.
Rnd 10 Knit.
Body
Rnds 11–14 With A and B held tog, work rnds 1–4 of leaf st.
Rnds 15–18 With B and C held tog, work rnds 1–4 of leaf st. Rep rnds 11–18 five (6) times more, then rnds 11–14 once.
Next rnd With A and B held tog, knit.
Ruffle
Change to one strand of D.
Rnd (inc) 1 *[Kf&b] twice, k4; rep from * around—160 (192) sts.
Rnds 2–4 Knit. Change to C.
Rnd 5 With C, purl. Change to D.
Rnd (eyelets) 6 With D, *k2tog tbl, yo; rep from * around. Change to A.
Rnd 7 With A, purl. Change to D and cont as foll:
Rnd 8 Knit.
Rnd (inc) 9 *[Kf&b] 4 times, k4; rep from * around—240 (288) sts.
Rnd 10 *K1, wrapping yarn twice around needle; rep from * around.
Rnd 11 Slip each st, dropping extra wrap.
Rnd 12 *K 2nd st on LH needle, then k first st, sl both sts from LH needle; rep from * around. Change to C.
Rnds 13–15 With C, knit. Change to D and cont as foll:
Rnd 16 *K1, wrapping yarn 3 times around needle; rep from * around.
Rnd 17 Slip each st, dropping extra wraps.
Rnd 18 Rep rnd 12.
Rnd 19 Knit. Bind off loosely knitwise. ✤

take a ribbing

Ribbing isn't just for edgings anymore, as this allover ribbed design demonstrates to dramatic effect.

take a ribbing

WHAT YOU NEED

Yarn
Mushishi **by Plymouth Yarn Company,
8¾oz/250g skeins, each approx
491yd/449m (wool/silk)** 🔵
• 2 (2, 2, 3) skeins in #06 granite

Needles
• **One size 7 (4.5mm) circular needle,
29"/74cm long,** or size to obtain gauge
• **Two size 7 (4.5mm) circular needles,
16"/40cm long**

Notions
• **Stitch markers**
• **Tapestry needle**
• **⅛"/3mm black leather lacing, 2yd/1.8m**

Skill Level
●●●●

RIBBED COWLNECK PULLOVER
Ribbing runs wild in this cropped pullover—
up and down the body, round the cowl, and
down the puffed sleeves. The variations in
the yarn play against the ribbing to add
more texture and visual interest.

SIZES
Instructions are written for size Small.
Changes for Medium, Large, and X-Large
are in parentheses. (Shown in size Small.)

FINISHED MEASUREMENTS
Bust at underarm 38 (40¾, 43½, 45½)"/96.5
(103.5, 110.5, 115.5)cm
Length 11½ (12¼, 13, 13¾)"/29 (31, 33, 35)cm

GAUGE
20 sts and 24 rows (rnds) to 4"/10cm over
k2, p2 rib using size 7 (4.5mm) circular
needle. **Take time to check gauge.**

NOTE
Pullover is worked in one piece from the
top down.

K2, P2 RIB
(over a multiple of 4 sts, worked back and
forth)
Row 1 *K2, p2; rep from * across.
Row 2 K the knit sts and p the purl sts.
Rep row 2 for k2, p2 rib.

K2, P2 RIB
(over a multiple of 4 sts plus 2, worked
back and forth)
Row 1 (RS) K2, *p2, k2; rep from * to end.
Row 2 P2, *k2, p2; rep from * to end.
Rep rows 1 and 2 for k2, p2 rib.

K2, P2 RIB
(over a multiple of 4 sts, worked in the rnd)
Rnd 1 *K2, p2; rep from * around.
Rep rnd 1 for k2, p2 rib.

PULLOVER
Neckline
Using 16"/40cm circular needle, cast on 52
(54, 56, 58) sts. Work back and forth.
Row 1 Knit.
Row 2 Purl.
Row 3 (RS) K 2 left front sts, pm, work 8
sleeve sts in k2, p2 rib, pm, work 32 (34, 36,
38) back sts in k2, p2 rib, pm, work 8 sleeve
sts in k2, p2 rib, pm, k 2 right front sts.
Row 4 (WS) K the knit sts and p the purl

sts as they appear, slipping markers.
Note Work all increases (yo's and cast-on
sts) into k2, p2 rib as established for each
section, including fronts, slipping markers
and changing to longer circular needle as
necessary.
Row (inc) 5 (RS) *Work rib as est to within 1
st of next marker, yo, k2, yo; rep from * 3
times more, work to end—60 (62, 64, 66) sts.
Row 6 (WS) Cast on 1 st, work in k2, p2 rib
as est across, cast on 1 st—62 (64, 66, 68) sts.
Rep rows 5 and 6 17 (18, 19, 20) times
more, ending with a WS row—232 (244,
256, 268) sts.
Cast on 2 (0, 2, 0) sts at beg of rnd. Pm for
beg of rnd for sizes Medium and X-Large
and between the 2 cast-on sts for Small and
Large.
Rnd (inc) 7 *Work k2, p2 rib to within 1 st
of next marker, yo, k2, yo; rep from * 3
times more, work rib to end—242 (252,
266, 276) sts.
Rnd 8 Work in rib as est. Rep rnds 7 and 8
ten (12, 13, 14) times more—322 (348, 370,
388) sts.
Divide yoke
Next rnd Bind off 50 (53, 57, 59) left front
sts, place 66 (72, 76, 80) sleeve sts on
16"/40cm circular needle and hold aside,
bind off 90 (98, 104, 110) back sts, place 66
(72, 76, 80) sleeve sts on 16"/40cm circular
needle and hold aside, bind off 50 (53, 57,
59) right front sts.
Sleeves
Using 66 (72, 76, 80) sleeve sts on 16"/40cm
circular needle, cast on 2 sts at underarm,
place a marker between the 2 sts, and join to
work in the rnd—68 (74, 78, 82) sts.
Rnds 1–3 Purl. **Rnds 4–6** Knit.
Rep rnds 1–6 eleven (12, 13, 14) times
more. Purl 1 rnd, decreasing 0 (2, 2, 2) sts
evenly around—68 (72, 76, 80) sts.
Work k2, p2 rib for 4 (4½, 4½, 5)"/10 (11.5,
11.5, 12.5)cm. Bind off in rib.
Rep for second sleeve.
Collar
Using 29"/74cm circular needle, pick up
120 (128, 136, 144) sts around neck edge.
Join and pm for beg of rnd.
Rnds 1–3 Knit. **Rnds 4–6** Purl.
Rep rnds 1–6 12 times more.
Next (picot) rnd *Yo, k2tog; rep from *
around. **Next rnd** Knit. Bind off.

FINISHING
Sew body and sleeves tog at the underarm.
Weave leather lacing in and out of picot
rnd beg and ending at center front collar. ❖

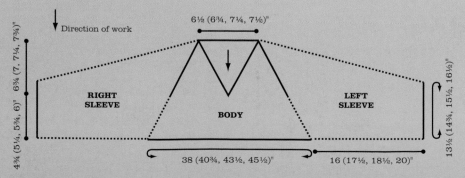

swing time

This swingy cardi is as fun and easy to knit as it is to wear.

swing time

WHAT YOU NEED

Yarn
Weekend **by Berroco, 3½oz/100g hanks, each approx 205yd/189m (acrylic/cotton)**
- 3 (3, 4, 5) hanks in #6902 vanilla (MC)
- 1 hank in #5934 pitch black (A)
- 1 hank in #5944 starry night (B)

Needles
- **One size 7 (4.5mm) circular needle, 24"/60cm long,** or size to obtain gauge
- **Two size 7 (4.5mm) circular needles, 16"/40cm long**

Notions
- **Stitch markers**
- **Tapestry needle**

Skill Level
●●●○

HORIZONTAL RIB CARDI
I designed this comfy coverup to be worn as a chic layer over pajamas, but it would look just as stylish about town. It works up quickly, so begin knitting in the morning and wear it that night!

SIZES
Instructions are written for size Small. Changes for Medium, Large, and X-Large are in parentheses. (Shown in size Small.)

FINISHED MEASUREMENTS
Back width at underarm 18 (20, 22, 24¼)"/45.5 (51, 56, 61.5)cm
Back length 11½ (12, 13½, 14)"/29 (30.5, 34.5, 35.5)cm

GAUGE
20 sts and 26 rows (rnds) to 4"/10cm over horizontal rib using size 7 (4.5mm) circular needle. **Take time to check gauge.**

NOTES
1) Cardigan is worked in one piece from the top down.
2) Schematic is on page 156.

HORIZONTAL RIB
(worked back and forth)
Row 1 (RS) Purl (ridge row).
Row 2 Purl.
Row 3 Knit.
Row 4 Purl.
Rep rows 1–4 for horizontal rib.

HORIZONTAL RIB
(worked in the round)
Rnds 1–3 Knit.
Rnd 4 Purl (ridge rnd).
Rep rnds 1–4 for horizontal rib.

CARDIGAN
Collar
Using color A and 16"/40cm circular needle, cast on 120 (124, 130, 134) sts. Work back and forth, changing to longer circular needle as needed.

Work 4 rows in St st (k on RS, p on WS). Change to MC and work 2 more rows.
Yoke
Beg horizontal rib and work 6 rows.
Next row (row 3 of pat st) K25, pm, k1, *yo, k2; rep from * 33 (35, 38, 40) times more, yo, k1, pm, k25—155 (161, 170, 176) sts.
Work 7 more rows in pat.
Next row (row 3 of pat st) K25, sl marker, k1, *yo, k3; rep from * 33 (35, 38, 40) times more, yo, k2, sl marker, k25—190 (198, 210, 218) sts.
Work 7 more rows in pat.
Next row (row 3 of pat st) K25, sl marker, k2, *yo, k4; rep from * 33 (35, 38, 40) times more, yo, k2, sl marker, k25—225 (235, 250, 260) sts.
Work 7 more rows in pat.
Next row (row 3 of pat st) K25, sl marker, k3, *yo, k5; rep from * 33 (35, 38, 40) times more, yo, k2, sl marker, k25—260 (272, 290, 302) sts.
Work 7 more rows in pat.
Next row (row 3 of pat st) K25, sl marker, k3, *yo, k6; rep from * 33 (35, 38, 40) times more, yo, k3, sl marker, k25—295 (309, 330, 344) sts.
Work 7 more rows in pat.
Next row (row 3 of pat st) K25, sl marker, k4, *yo, k7; rep from * 33 (35, 38, 40) times, yo, k3, sl marker, k25—330 (346, 370, 386) sts.
For size Small only
Cont to work in horizontal rib until drop from neckline measures 8"/20.5cm, ending with row 2. Cont to yoke divide.
For sizes Medium, Large, and X-Large
Work 7 more rows in pat.
Next row (row 3 of pat st) K25, sl marker, *yo, k (21, 16, 10); rep from * across, k (2, 0, 6) sts to panel marker, sl marker, k25—(360, 390, 419) sts.
Continue to work in horizontal rib until drop from neckline measures (8¼, 9, 9½)"/(21.5, 23, 24)cm, ending with row 2. Cont to yoke divide.
Divide yoke (all sizes)
K 65 (70, 75, 79) left front sts, cast on 2 sts at underarm, place 55 (60, 65, 70)

sleeve sts onto a 16"/40cm circular needle and hold aside, k 90 (100, 110, 121) back sts, cast on 2 sts at underarm, place 55 (60, 65, 70) sleeve sts onto a 16"/40cm circular needle and hold aside, k 65 (70, 75, 79) right front sts—224 (244, 264, 283) sts remain.

Body
Cont in est horizontal rib until body measures 3½ (3½, 4½, 4½)"/9 (9, 11.5, 11.5)cm from underarm, ending with row 1. Change to B and work 4 rows in St st. Bind off.

Sleeves
Using MC and 55 (60, 65, 70) sleeve sts on circular needle, pm at underarm and join to beg working in the rnd. Beg horizontal rib pat in the rnd. *Work 2 rnds in MC. Change to A and work 2 rnds. Change to MC and work 2 rnds. Change to B and work 2 rnds; rep from * 5 (5, 6, 6) times more. Change to MC. Knit 4 rnds. Bind off.
Rep for second sleeve.

FINISHING
Use tapestry needle to sew body and sleeves together at underarm. Weave in remaining ends.

Front edges
Fold (25 st) front panel inward and in half, baste to inside, taking a st at each ridge row.

Front ties (make 2)
Measure out 6 (2 of each color) 1-yd lengths of yarn. Holding the ends together, make a knot at one end, leaving a half-inch tail. Thread the 6-ply bunch of thread into a tapestry needle. Counting 4–5 ridges down from the top front of the sweater, from the front side poke the tapestry needle into the sweater about an inch from the edge and from the back side poke it up through the front about a half-inch toward the edge; tie another knot closely to the fabric. Take out the tapestry needle and tie knots down the remaining length of the yarns about every inch. Repeat for other side. ❖

shawl we dance?

You'll be the belle of the ball any way
you wear this versatile wrap.

shawl we dance?

WHAT YOU NEED

Yarn
Vintage Chunky **by Berroco, 3½oz/100g
balls, each approx 130yd/120m
(acrylic/wool/nylon)**
• **4 balls in #6185 tide pool (A)**
• **1 ball each in #6194 breezeway (B)
and #6134 sour cherry (D)**
• **2 balls each in #6121 sunny (C) and
#6105 oats (E)**

Needles
• **Size 8 (5mm) circular needles,
16"/40cm and 24"/61cm long,** or size to
obtain gauge
• **Size 10½ (6.5mm) circular needle,
29"/74cm long,** or size to obtain gauge
• **One size 8 (5mm) double-pointed
needles (dpns)**

Notions
• **Stitch marker**

Skill Level
● ● ● ●

SHAWL-COLLAR PONCHO

This abbreviated poncho starts with an
overlapping ribbed collar, which can be
gathered around the neck and pinned or
folded over to encompass the shoulders.
The tweedy-looking body is created by
working multiple colors in seed stitch.

SIZE
Instructions are written for one size fits
most.

FINISHED MEASUREMENTS
Bottom circumference 44"/111.5cm
Length (including neckband) 15½"/39.5cm

GAUGES
18 sts and 23 rows to 4"/10cm over k3,
p3 rib using 1 strand of yarn and
smaller circular needle (slightly
stretched).
11 sts and 21 rnds to 4"/10cm over seed
st using 2 strands of yarn held tog and
larger circular needle. **Take time to
check gauges.**

NOTES
1) Use one strand of yarn for ribbed
outer layer of capelet and 2 strands held
tog for seed-stitch underlayer.
2) Capelet is worked in one piece from
bottom edge of ribbed outer layer up to
neckband, then from neckband down to
bottom edge of seed-stitch underlayer.

K3, P3 RIB
(over a multiple of 6 sts plus 3)
Row 1 (RS) K3, *p3, k3; rep from * to
end.
Row 2 P3, *k3, p3; rep from * to end.
Rep rows 1 and 2 for k3, p3 rib.

SEED STITCH
(over a multiple of 2 sts)
Rnd 1 *K1, p1; rep from * around.
Rnd 2 K the purl sts and p the knit sts.
Rep rnd 2 for seed st.

CAPELET

Ribbed outer layer
Beg at bottom edge, with smaller, longer
circular needle and A, cast on 303 sts.
Work back and forth in k3, p3 rib for
8"/20.5cm, end with a WS row.
Dec row (RS) K1, *k2tog tbl; rep from *
to end—152 sts.
Next row Purl.
Joining overlap
Place 32 sts at opposite end from
working yarn onto dpn. With RS
facing, bring sts on dpn around to WS of
sts on circular needle (forming a circle),
and so RH end of dpn and LH end of
circular needle are parallel.
Next (joining) rnd Insert RH end of
circular needle knitwise into first st of
each needle and wrap yarn around each
needle as if to knit, then knit these 2 sts
tog and sl them off the needles. *K the
next 2 sts tog in the same manner; rep
from * 30 times more, then knit to end of
rnd—120 sts. Pm for beg of rnds.
Neckband
Work around in k1, p1 rib for 3½"/9cm.
Next rnd Knit.
Seed-st underlayer
Change to larger circular needle. Cont in
seed st and work in stripe pat as foll:
Rnd 1 Use B and E held tog.
Rnd 2 Use C and E held tog.
Rnd 3 Use D and E held tog. Rep these 3
rnds for 10¼"/26.5cm. Cont in stripe pat
as foll:
Rnd 1 Use B and C held tog.
Rnd 2 Use C and D held tog. Rep these 2
rnds for 3"/7.5cm. Bind off loosely
knitwise.

FINISHING
Position ribbed outer layer on top of seed
st under layer, folding neckband in half.
Using A, sew first and last rnds of
neckband tog using a running st. ❖

café con leche

A two-toned neutral palette and a richly textured stitch pattern
create a delicious look for any fashion taste.

café con leche

WHAT YOU NEED

Yarn
Bonsai **by Berroco, 1¾oz/50g hanks,
each approx 77yd/71m (bamboo/nylon)** (4)
• 5 (5, 6, 6) hanks in #4112 kinoko (A)
• 3 (3, 3, 4) hanks in #4103 bamboo (B)

Needles
• **Two size 7 (4.5mm) circular needles,
29"/74cm long,** or size to obtain gauge
• **Cable needle (cn)**

Notions
• **Stitch markers**

Skill Level
●●●○

DROP-STITCH CROP TOP

I chose a lacy drop-stitch pattern to show off the ribbon-like shape of Berroco's **Bonsai** yarn. Tape yarns like these are fun and quick to knit. The easy shape of this top flatters any wearer.

SIZES

Instructions are written for size Small. Changes for Medium, Large, and X-Large are in parentheses. (Shown in size Small.)

FINISHED MEASUREMENTS

Bust 36 (40, 44, 47½)"/91.5 (101.5, 111.5, 120.5)cm
Length 10 (10, 12, 12)"/25.5 (25.5, 30.5, 30.5)cm
Upper arm 20 (20, 24, 24)"/51 (51, 61, 61)cm

GAUGE

17 sts and 28 rows to 4"/10cm over drop cross st using size 7 (4.5mm) circular needle. **Take time to check gauge.**

NOTE

Back and front are each worked from the neck down.

DROP CROSS STITCH

(over a multiple of 6 sts)
For gauge swatch, cast on 18 sts.
Rows 1–4 Knit.
Row 5 (WS) *K1 wrapping yarn 3 times around needle; rep from * to end. Slip sts to 2nd circular needle, dropping extra wraps. Cont as foll:
Row 6 (RS) *Sl 3 sts to cn and hold to **front**, k3, k3 from cn; rep from * to end.
Rows 7–10 Knit.
Row 11 (WS) *K1, wrapping yarn 3 times around needle; rep from * to end. Slip sts to 2nd circular needle, dropping extra wraps. Cont as foll:

Row 12 (RS) *Sl 3 sts to cn and hold to **back**, k3, k3 from cn; rep from * to end. Rep rows 1–12 once more, then rows 1–4. Bind off knitwise. Piece should measure 4"/10cm square.

BACK

Beg at neck edge, with A, cast on 120 (132, 144, 156) sts. Cont in drop cross st as foll:
Rows 1–4 Knit.
Row 5 (WS) K3 (garter st border), pm, *k1, wrapping yarn 3 times around needle; rep from * to last 3 sts, pm, k3 (garter st border). Slip sts (and markers) to 2nd circular needle, dropping extra wraps. Cont as foll:
Row 6 (RS) K3, sl marker, *sl 3 sts to cn and hold to **front**, k3, k3 from cn; rep from * to marker, sl marker, k3.
Rows 7–10 Knit.
Row 11 (WS) K3, sl marker, *k1, wrapping yarn 3 times around needle; rep from * to marker, sl marker, k3. Slip sts (and markers) to 2nd circular needle, dropping extra wraps. Cont as foll:
Row 12 (RS) K3, sl marker, *sl 3 sts to cn and hold to **back**, k3, k3 from cn; rep from * to marker, sl marker, k3.
Rows 13–16 Knit. Slipping markers every row, rep rows 5–16 four (4, 5, 5) times more. Bind off loosely knitwise.

FRONT

Work as for back until rows 1–15 have been completed, end with a WS row. Change to B. Work row 16. With B, cont to rep rows 5–16 four (4, 5, 5) times more. Bind off loosely knitwise.

FINISHING

Sew a 9 (10, 11, 12)"/23 (25.5, 28, 30.5)cm shoulder seam each side. Sew a 5 (5½, 6, 6½)"/12.5 (14, 15, 16.5)cm sleeve seam each side. ❖

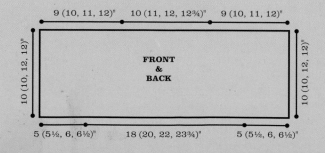

9 (10, 11, 12)"   10 (11, 12, 12¾)"   9 (10, 11, 12)"

10 (10, 12, 12)"

**FRONT
&
BACK**

10 (10, 12, 12)"

5 (5½, 6, 6½)"   18 (20, 22, 23¾)"   5 (5½, 6, 6½)"

mo' better blues

Several mohair yarns in shades of blue combine to create a wrap
that is the ultimate in sumptuous texture and color.

mo' better blues

WHAT YOU NEED

Yarn

African Bead Ball **by Be Sweet**, 1¾oz/50g balls, each approx 60yd/55m (baby mohair/metallic/hand-tied glass beads)

• 1 (2, 2, 2) ball in #19ab dark denim (A)

Brushed Mohair **by Be Sweet**, 1¾oz/50g balls, each approx 120yd/110m (baby mohair) ⑤

• 2 (3, 3, 3) balls each in #17 sea green (B), #28 deep turquoise (C), #17a lichen (D), #20 navy (E), and #28c lapis (F)

Needles

• **Two size 10 (6mm) circular needles, 29"/74cm long,** or size to obtain gauge
• **One set (5) size 10 (6mm) double-pointed needles (dpns)**

Notions

• Stitch holders
• Stitch marker
• One 1"/25mm button

Skill Level

●●●○

SCARF-FRONT SHRUG

Mohair is high on my list of yummy must-use yarns. I love its raw yet fluffy texture and the wide range of colors it comes in. For this shrug, I elongated the front to create a scarf that wraps around the neck and tucks into the front. It's both dramatic and extremely wearable.

SIZES

Instructions are written for size Small. Changes for Medium, Large, and X-Large are in parentheses. (Shown in size Small.)

FINISHED MEASUREMENTS

Bust (closed) 36 (38½, 42½, 45)"/91.5 (98, 108, 114.5)cm

Length 10(10¾, 11½, 12)"/25.5 (27.5, 29, 30.5)cm

Upper arm 15 (16¼, 17½, 18¾)"/38 (41, 44.5, 47.5)cm

GAUGE

16 sts to 5"/12.5cm and 22 rows to 4"/10cm over garter st using size 10 (6mm) circular needle. **Take time to check gauge.**

NOTE

Shrug is worked in one piece from the neckband down.

SHRUG

Neckband

With circular needle and using the backward loop method, cast on 202 (209, 219, 226) sts, alternating between C and E. Work back and forth using 2 circular needles as foll:

Next 2 rows With E, knit.

Next 2 rows With A, knit.

Next (buttonhole) row (RS) With C, k3, bind off next 2 sts, knit to end.

Next row With C, knit across, casting on 2 sts over bound-off sts.

Yoke

Next row (RS) With D, k 20 (22, 24, 26) sts (left front), pm, k6 sts (left sleeve), pm, k 16 (16, 18, 18) sts (back), pm, k6 sts (right sleeve), pm, k 154 (159, 165, 170) sts (right front and scarf).

Next row With D, knit. Cont in garter st (knit every row) and stripe pat (2 rows each E, F, B, C, and D), work as foll:

Inc row (RS) *Knit to 1 st before next marker, yo, k1, slip marker, k1, yo; rep from * 3 times more, knit to end.

Next row Knit. Rep last 2 rows 19 (21, 23, 25) times more, end with a WS row—362 (385, 411, 434) sts.

Divide for body and sleeves

Next row (RS) With next color, k 40 (44, 48, 52) sts (left front), cast on 2 sts (underarm), place next 46 (50, 54, 58) sts on holder for left sleeve, k 56 (60, 66, 70) sts (back), cast on 2 sts (underarm), place next 46 (50, 54, 58) sts on holder for right sleeve, k 174 (181, 189, 196) sts (right front and scarf)—274 (289, 307, 322) sts.

Next row With same color as last row, knit. (Make note of what color was used for last 2 rows to work sleeves.)

Next 2 rows With A, knit. **Next 2 rows** With next color, knit. Bind off knitwise, alternating between next 2 colors.

Sleeves

With RS facing, dpn, and color used to divide for body and sleeves, k 46 (50, 54, 58) sts from sleeve holder, cast on 1 st, pm for beg of rnds, cast on 1 st—48 (52, 56, 60) sts. Divide sts evenly over 4 needles. Join to work in rnds. Mark last rnd.

Next rnd With same color, purl. Cont in garter st (knit 1 rnd, purl 1 rnd) and stripe pat as established, work even until piece measures 17 (17½, 18, 18½)"/43 (44.5, 45.5, 47)cm above marked row, end with a purl rnd. **Next rnd** With A, knit.

Next rnd With A, purl.

Next rnd With next color, knit.

Next rnd With same color as last rnd, purl. Bind off knitwise, alternating between next 2 colors.

FINISHING

Sew cast-on sts of underarms tog. Sew button to WS of upper right front to correspond to buttonhole. ❖

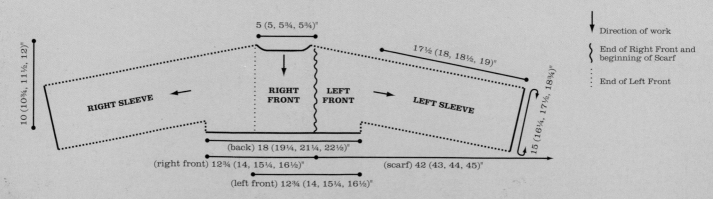

schematics & charts

out of the blue
(Pattern on pages 14–17.)

↓ Direction of work

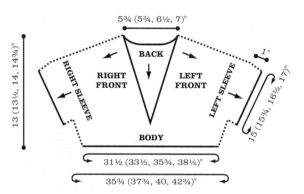

5¾ (5¾, 6½, 7)"

BACK

RIGHT FRONT   LEFT FRONT

RIGHT SLEEVE

LEFT SLEEVE

BODY

1"

13 (13½, 14, 14¾)"

15 (15¾, 16½, 17)"

31½ (33½, 35¾, 38½)"

35¾ (37¾, 40, 42¾)"

tee time
(Pattern on pages 46–49.)

↓ Direction of work

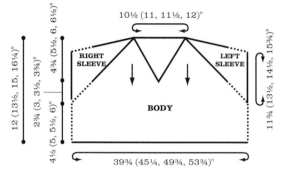

10½ (11, 11½, 12)"

RIGHT SLEEVE   LEFT SLEEVE

BODY

12 (13½, 15, 16¼)"

4¾ (5½, 6, 6½)"

2¾ (3, 3½, 3¾)"

4½ (5, 5½, 6)"

11¾ (13½, 14½, 15¾)"

39¾ (45¼, 49¾, 53¾)"

tie one on
(Pattern on pages 18–21.)

↓ Direction of work

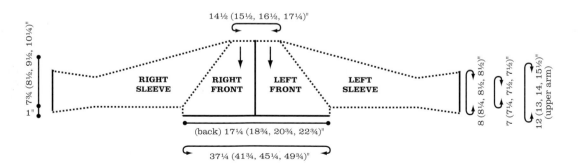

14½ (15½, 16½, 17¼)"

RIGHT SLEEVE   RIGHT FRONT   LEFT FRONT   LEFT SLEEVE

7¾ (8½, 9½, 10¼)"

1"

8 (8¼, 8½, 8½)"

7 (7¼, 7½, 7½)"

12 (13, 14, 15½)" (upper arm)

(back) 17¼ (18¾, 20¾, 22¾)"

37¼ (41¾, 45¼, 49¾)"

all tucked in
(Pattern on pages 62–65.)

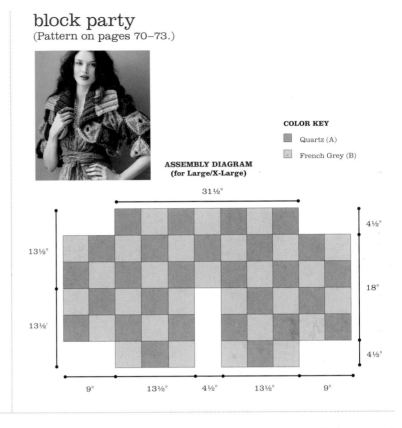

↓ Direction of work

· · · Stitching line on WS for neckband and sleeve hems

17 (18, 19, 20)"

YOKE

BODY

13½ (14, 14¼, 15)"

1¼"

13 (14, 15, 16)"

36 (40, 44, 48)"

block party
(Pattern on pages 70–73.)

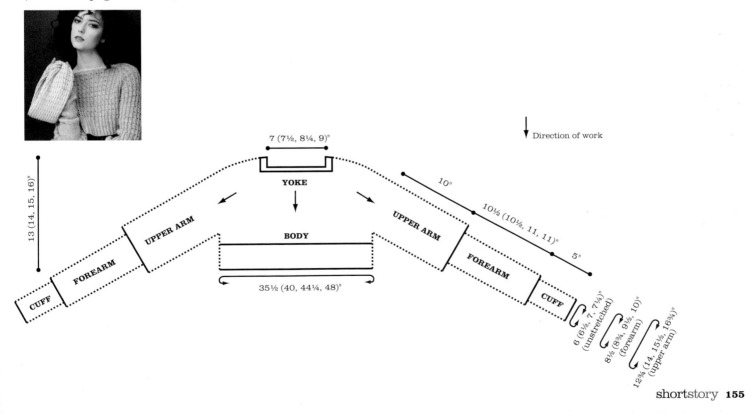

COLOR KEY

■ Quartz (A)

□ French Grey (B)

ASSEMBLY DIAGRAM
(for Large/X-Large)

31½"

4½"

18"

4½"

13½"

13½'

9"   13½"   4½"   13½"   9"

silver lining
(Pattern on pages 102–105.)

7 (7½, 8¼, 9)"

YOKE

↓ Direction of work

13 (14, 15, 16)"

UPPER ARM

FOREARM

CUFF

BODY

UPPER ARM

FOREARM

CUFF

10"

10½ (10½, 11, 11)"

5"

35½ (40, 44¼, 48)"

6 (6½, 7, 7½)" (unstretched)

8½ (8¾, 9½, 10)" (forearm)

12¾ (14, 15½, 16¾)" (upper arm)

schematics & charts

bold & beautiful
(Pattern on pages 110–113.)

CHART 1

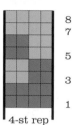

8
7
5
3
1

4-st rep

CHART 2

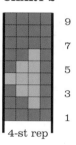

9
7
5
3
1

4-st rep

CHART 3

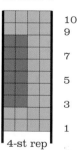

10
9
7
5
3
1

4-st rep

CHART 4

4
3
1

4-st rep

CHART 5

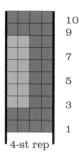

10
9
7
5
3
1

4-st rep

CHART 6

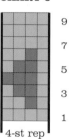

9
7
5
3
1

4-st rep

COLOR KEY

■ Regal Red (A)

■ Blue Hawaii (B)

swing time
(Pattern on pages 138–141.)

↓ Direction of work

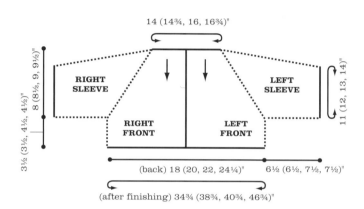

14 (14¾, 16, 16¾)"

RIGHT SLEEVE

LEFT SLEEVE

RIGHT FRONT

LEFT FRONT

3½ (3½, 4½, 4½)"

8 (8½, 9, 9½)"

11 (12, 13, 14)"

(back) 18 (20, 22, 24¼)"

6½ (6½, 7½, 7½)"

(after finishing) 34¾ (38¾, 40¾, 46¾)"

abbreviations

approx	approximately
beg	begin(ning)
CC	contrasting color
ch	chain
cm	centimeter(s)
cn	cable needle
cont	continu(e)(ing)
dec	decreas(e)(ing)
dpn(s)	double-pointed needle(s)
foll	follow(s)(ing)
g	gram(s)
inc	increas(e)(ing)
k	knit
kfb	knit into front and back of stitch
k2tog	knit 2 stitches together
LH	left-hand
lp(s)	loop(s)
m	meter(s)
MB	make bobble
MC	main color
mm	millimeter(s)
M1	make one: with needle tip, lift strand between last stitch knit (purled) and the next stitch on the LH needle and knit (purl) into back of it
oz	ounce(s)
p	purl
pat(s)	pattern(s)
pm	place marker
psso	pass slip stitch(es) over
p2tog	purl 2 stitches together
rem	remain(s)(ing)
rep	repeat
RH	right-hand
rnd(s)	round(s)
RS	right side(s)
S2KP	slip 2 stitches together, knit 1, pass 2 slip stitches over knit 1
SKP	slip 1, knit 1, pass slip stitch over
SK2P	slip 1, knit 2 together, pass slip stitch over the knit 2 together
sl	slip
sl st	slip stitch
ssk (ssp)	slip next 2 stitches knitwise (purlwise), one at a time; knit (purl) these 2 stitches tog
sssk	slip next 3 stitches knitwise, one at a time; knit these 3 stitches tog
st(s)	stitch(es)
St st	stockinette stitch
tbl	through back loop(s)
tog	together
WS	wrong side(s)
wyib	with yarn in back
wyif	with yarn in front
yd	yard(s)
yo	yarn over needle
*	repeat directions following * as many times as indicated
[ ]	repeat directions inside brackets as many times as indicated

techniques

Yarn Overs

Between two knit stitches: Bring the yarn from the back of the work to the front between the two needles. Knit the next stitch, bringing the yarn to the back over the right-hand needle, as shown.

Between two purl stitches: Leave the yarn at the front of the work. Bring the yarn to the back over the right-hand needle and to the front again, as shown. Purl the next stitch.

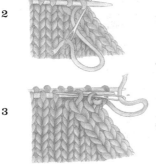

Kitchener Stitch

1. Insert tapestry needle purlwise (as shown) through first stitch on front needle. Pull yarn through, leaving that stitch on knitting needle.

2. Insert tapestry needle knitwise (as shown) through first stitch on back needle. Pull yarn through, leaving stitch on knitting needle.

3. Insert tapestry needle knitwise through first stitch on front needle, slip stitch off needle and insert tapestry needle purlwise (as shown) through next stitch on front needle. Pull yarn through, leaving this stitch on needle.

4. Insert tapestry needle purlwise through first stitch on back needle. Slip stitch off needle and insert tapestry needle knitwise (as shown) through next stitch on back needle. Pull yarn through, leaving this stitch on needle.

Repeat steps 3 and 4 until all stitches on both front and back needles have been grafted. Fasten off and weave in end.

1

2

3

4

I-cord

Cast on about three to five sitches. *Knit one row. Without turning the work, slip the stitches back to the beginning of the row. Pull the yarn tightly from the end of the row. Repeat from the * as desired. Bind off.

3-Needle Bind-off

1. With the right side of the two pieces facing each other, and the needles parallel, insert a third needle knitwise into the first stitch of each needle. Wrap the yarn around the needle as if to knit.

2. Knit these two stitches together and slip them off the needles. *Knit the next two stitches together in the same way as shown.

3. Slip the first stitch on the third needle over the second stitch and off the needle. Repeat from the * in step 2 across the row until all the stitches are bound off.

Tassels

Cut yarn twice desired length, plus extra for knotting. On WS, insert hook from front to back through piece and over folded yarn. Pull yarn through. Draw ends through and tighten. Trim yarn.

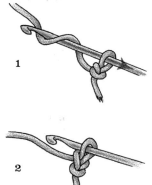

Crochet Chain Stitch

1. Make a slip knot near the end of the hook, then wrap the working yarn (the yarn attached to the ball or skein) around the hook as shown. Draw the yarn through the loop on the hook by catching it with the hook and pulling it toward you.

2. One chain stitch is complete. Repeat to create as many chain stitches as required, adding beads between stitches if desired.

Cable Cast-on

1. Make a slip knot on the left needle. Insert the right needle knitwise into the stitch on the left needle. Wrap the yarn around the right needle as if to knit.

2. Draw the yarn through the first stitch to make a new stitch, but do not drop the stitch from the left needle.

3. Slip the new stitch to the left needle as shown.

4. Insert the right needle between the two stitches on the left needle.

5. Wrap the yarn around the right needle as if to knit and pull the yarn through to make a new stitch.

6. Place the new stitch on the left needle as shown. Repeat steps 4 through 6 to cast on the desired number of stitches.

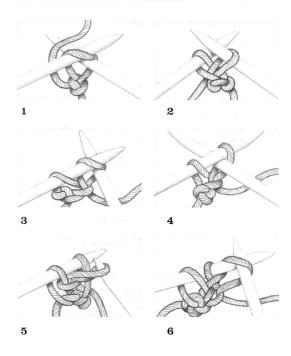

resources

Berroco Inc.
1 Tupperware Drive, Suite 4
North Smithfield, RI 02896
www.berroco.com

Be Sweet
1315 Bridgeway
Sausalito, CA 94965
www.besweetproducts.com

Blue Sky Alpacas, Inc.
P.O. Box 88
Cedar, MN 55011
www.blueskyalpacas.com

Brown Sheep Company
100662 County Road 16
Mitchell, NE 69357
www.brownsheep.com

Cascade Yarns
1224 Andover Park East
Tukwila, WA 98188
www.cascadeyarns.com

Catskill Merino
www.catskill-merino.com

Classic Elite Yarns
122 Western Avenue
Lowell, MA 01851
www.classiceliteyarns.com

Colinette Yarns
Banwy Workshops, Units 2-5
Llanfair Caereinion
Powy, Wales, SY21 0SG
Tel: 01938-810128

Debbie Bliss
Distributed by Knitting Fever
www.debbieblissonline.com

Filatura di Crosa
Distributed by
Tahki·Stacy Charles, Inc.

Hamilton Design
Storgatan 14
64730 Mariefred, Sweden
Tel/Fax: +46 (0) 159-12006
www.hamiltondesign.biz

Jade Sapphire Exotic Fibres
Tel: (866) 857-3897
www.jadesapphire.com

Jil Eaton Yarns
Distributed by
Classic Elite Yarns
www.classiceliteyarns.com

Knitting Fever (KFI)
P.O. Box 336
315 Bayview Avenue
Amityville, NY 11701
www.knittingfever.com

Lion Brand Yarn Co.
34 West 15th Street
New York, NY 10011
www.lionbrand.com

Misti Alpaca Yarns
In the U.S.:
P.O. Box 2532
Glen Ellyn, Illinois 60138
www.mistialpaca.com
In Canada:
Old Mill Knitting Company
F.G. P.O. Box 81176
Ancaster, Ontario L9G 4X2
www.oldmillknitting.com

Plymouth Yarn Co.
500 Lafayette Street
Bristol, PA 19007
www.plymouthyarn.com

Quince & Co.
www.quinceandco.com

Rowan
www.knitrowan.com
In the U.S.:
Distributed by Westminster
Fibers, Inc.
In the U.K.:
Green Lane Mill Holmfirth,
West Yorkshire
HD9 2DX

S. Charles Collezione
Distributed by
Tahki·Stacy Charles, Inc.

Tahki·Stacy Charles, Inc.
70-60 83rd Street,
Building #12
Glendale, NY 11385
www.tahkistacycharles.com

Tahki Yarns
Distributed by
Tahki·Stacy Charles, Inc.

Tanglewood Fiber Creations
www.tanglewoodfibercreations.com

Tilli Tomas
Tel: (617) 524-3330
www.tillitomas.com

Westminster Fibers, Inc.
165 Ledge Street
Nashua, NH 03060
www.westminsterfibers.com

standard yarn weight system

Categories of yarn, gauge ranges, and recommended needle and hook sizes

Yarn Weight Symbol & Category Names	**0** Lace	**1** Super Fine	**2** Fine	**3** Light	**4** Medium	**5** Bulky	**6** Super Bulky
Type of Yarns in Category	Fingering 10 count crochet thread	Sock, Fingering, Baby	Sport, Baby	DK, Light Worsted	Worsted, Afghan, Aran	Chunky, Craft, Rug	Bulky, Roving
Knit Gauge Range* in Stockinette Stitch to 4 inches	33–40** sts	27–32 sts	23–26 sts	21–24 sts	16–20 sts	12–15 sts	6–11 sts
Recommended Needle in Metric Size Range	1.5–2.25 mm	2.25–3.25 mm	3.25–3.75 mm	3.75–4.5 mm	4.5–5.5 mm	5.5–8 mm	8 mm and larger
Recommended Needle U.S. Size Range	000 to 1	1 to 3	3 to 5	5 to 7	7 to 9	9 to 11	11 and larger
Crochet Gauge* Ranges in Single Crochet to 4 inch	32–42 double crochets**	21–32 sts	16–20 sts	12–17 sts	11–14 sts	8–11 sts	5–9 sts
Recommended Hook in Metric Size Range	Steel*** 1.6–1.4mm Regular hook 2.25 mm	2.25–3.5 mm	3.5–4.5 mm	4.5–5.5 mm	5.5–6.5 mm	6.5–9 mm	9 mm and larger
Recommended Hook U.S. Size Range	Steel*** 6, 7, 8 Regular hook B–1	B–1 to E–4	E–4 to 7	7 to I–9	I–9 to K–10½	K–10½ to M–13	M–13 and larger

* GUIDELINES ONLY: The above reflect the most commonly used gauges and needle or hook sizes for specific yarn categories.

** Lace weight yarns are usually knitted or crocheted on larger needles and hooks to create lacy, openwork patterns. Accordingly, a gauge range is difficult to determine. Always follow the gauge stated in your pattern.

*** Steel crochet hooks are sized differently from regular hooks--the higher the number, the smaller the hook, which is the reverse of regular hook sizing.

This Standards & Guidelines booklet and downloadable symbol artwork are available at: **YarnStandards.com**

skill levels for knitting

● ○ ○ ○   ● ● ○ ○   ● ● ● ○   ● ● ● ●

Beginner
Ideal first
project.

Easy
Basic stitches,
minimal
shaping,
simple
finishing.

Intermediate
For knitters
with some
experience.
More intricate
stitches,
shaping, and
finishing.

Experienced
For knitters
able to work
patterns with
complicated
shaping and
finishing.

index